RUINS AND FOLLIES
OF EAST ANGLIA

Edward Couzens-Lake

AMBERLEY

First published 2019

Amberley Publishing
The Hill, Stroud
Gloucestershire, GL5 4EP

www.amberleybooks.com

British Library Cataloguing in Publication Data.
A catalogue record for this book is available from the British Library.

ISBN 978 1 4456 7298 4 (print)
ISBN 978 1 4456 7299 1 (ebook)

Typesetting and Origination by Amberley Publishing.
Printed in Great Britain.

Contents

Introduction

I am not a historian.

I have the greatest respect for the men and women that have dedicated their lives to the rigorous study and research demanded of exploring and explaining our past. It would be no exaggeration to say that I am even in awe of some of them. Maybe if I'd studied the right subjects at university, I might have been a historian myself.

Had I done so and still written this book then it would, no doubt, have been full of historical facts and figures. But then it also might have ended up as a rather too concise piece of work, one overflowing with the historical minutiae that embrace each of the special sites I have chosen within these pages.

But as I am not a historian you can rest assured that this book only flirts with that sort of discipline.

What I most definitely am is a dreamer; an explorer and inescapable romantic, a man who lets his heart rule his head, one who seeks story and wonder in everything he sees.

Which is exactly the approach I have taken with regard to the ruins and follies featured here. So, at the risk of losing a sale, if you are flicking through this book in a shop hoping for factually rich accounts relating to some of East Anglia's quirkier and ancient sites then this might not be what you are looking for.

This book is intended to accompany the reader on their visits to the places listed. Hopefully they will encourage you to lose yourself in some of them, just as I was able to do myself, even if some of them are not accessible, dangerous or on privately owned land. What's important is for you to use your imagination as you explore or espy each of these sights. Our imaginations are an underused and unvalued resource, the joys of which are all too easily lost as we grow up. To you and me a cardboard box is a cardboard box, a receptacle for carrying things in, something functional and lifeless. Yet, to a child, it can be a ship, a tank or a spacecraft; there are no limits to the places that a simple box can take them to.

So why not indulge in the same riot of imagination when you explore the ruins of an old church or feast your heart and mind upon a building that was designed and built in the manner it was simply because someone wanted form and function to be replaced by flair and fantasy?

When you open the door of a folly, you also, just as its architect did, open one to the imagination.

Let yours have a treat within these pages and places.

Edward Couzens-Lake

Chapter 1

Aldeburgh

Scallop

Art is meant to be controversial. Artists crave for their work to be talked about, to promote and provoke discourse, praise and criticism. Yes, even criticism. The worst thing that can ever happen to an artist is for a piece of work to be completely ignored and disregarded. For them even a negative reaction is better than none at all for, as Oscar Wilde famously said, 'There is only one thing in life worse than being talked about, and that is not being talked about.'

Artists are no different to writers. They'd rather their work was talked about, even if that talk is not always complimentary in nature.

Maggi Hambling is a painter and sculptor who, appropriately, created a sculpture entitled *A Conversation With Oscar Wilde* in 1998. It didn't go down particularly well with the art cognoscenti upon its unveiling, with one critic likening it to a Madam Tussauds waxwork. *Scallop*, her 15-foot-high tribute to Benjamin Britten, which stands on the beach at Aldeburgh, was also subjected to criticism when it was unveiled in 2003, with some local residents going as far as raising petitions demanding the sculpture's immediate removal from the beach. *Scallop* has also been vandalised on numerous occasions, including one attack in 2012, which saw the words 'It's an old tin can' painted onto it.

Whatever you might think of it (and *Scallop* has as many supporters as it does detractors) the piece is most certainly eye-catchingly impressive. The fact that it stands in such splendid isolation on a beach means, of course, that it is as open to unwanted attention as it is to the elements but surely the fact that it has garnished such a reaction is justification for its existence and evidence of a job well done by its creator?

Great art is accessible. You should be able to touch it, sit on it, climb all over it and pose for a selfie as you lean against it. Try that with Michelangelo's *David* and see where it gets you. On second thoughts, please don't. I don't want anyone spending a few night in a Florence *prigione* on my account.

And look, don't feel compelled to have a pop at *Scallop* either. Hate it if you like but, rather than feel compelled to damage it, ask yourself why it provokes such a strong reaction in you and, with that being the case, congratulate its creator for ticking one of your boxes rather than leaving it blank and unanswered.

Hambling wanted *Scallop* to share that wild and oft-untamed eastern coast of England that had so inspired Britten, a composer who draws similar levels of both light and shadow from assorted admirers and critics of his work. The sculpture is pierced with a quote from Britten's opera *Peter Grimes*: 'I hear those voices that will not be drowned.'

Scallop, like those voices, will forever be inundated by both the sea and the harshest of words and actions of those who judge it. But it will never drown.

(David Dixon at Geograph.org.uk)

Chapter 2

Aldeburgh

Lookout Towers

Countless brave men and women have taken to the seas around the British shores and beyond for an almost infinite variety of reasons: defence, trade, fishing, leisure and scientific. And for hundreds of years. The resources, motivations and craft that the very earliest of seafarers might have had is completely different to those available to the twenty-first-century sailor. Yet, the one thing that they have in common is that shared respect of the sea. She can be the most vengeful of mistresses.

The waters off the East Anglian shores might almost be regarded as relatively benign by the unwary and ill-advised. But that is not the case and woe to thee if you are thinking of taking to them without the sort of supervision, training and safety equipment demanded as standard.

For those who have sailed the waters off the Suffolk coast, it has always been reassuring to know that expert assistance is always at hand if needed. Braver than the brave are those who take to the sea in order to save the lives of those whom she has seen fit to play with in a fit of pique and storm. This reassurance has been provided by the RNLI station that evolved from the original Suffolk Shipwreck Association station in 1851. Aldeburgh has had a lifeboat ever since.

Prior to the coming of the RNLI, the beaches were observed from two lookout towers known, simply, as the North and South lookouts. These were occupied by two rival companies whose roles were, rather than primarily saving lives, to eke out a living from the ships sailing the nearby waters by offering a variety of services for the huge number and variety of sailing boats that might be navigating the waters off that stretch of coast at any given time. One of these was most certainly as willing lifeboatmen for any craft that might have found itself in distress and in need of assistance.

Needless to say, these enterprising individuals would also make themselves available as salvage men if, for whatever reasons, a ship and its cargo could not be rescued at sea and was lost, although they would always try to save lives if they possibly could. In that respect, therefore, they are the courageous forerunners to those men and women who would eventually work as volunteers for the RNLI at Aldeburgh.

Of the two towers that still stand at Aldeburgh, the South Tower is now used as a thriving arts centre (see *www.aldeburghbeachlookout.com*), while the lower part of the North Tower houses the RNLI's current inshore lifeboat. It dates from the mid-nineteenth century and features white brick quoins (decorative features on the corners of a building intended to reinforce an onlooker's sense of a structure's presence and strength) and bands. The tower roof is in the shape of a pyramid with a white brick dentil (a small block used as a repeating ornament-type piece) cornice, the use of dentils here a nod by the designers to classical Greek and Roman architecture where they are commonly found: strength and permanence giving reassurance.

(Ray Blyth)

Chapter 3

Babingley

St Felix's Church

There always seems to be something particularly evocative about the ruins of a church, however humble it might have been in its heyday – or, for that matter, grand. The city of Coventry's modern cathedral is modernist in design and symbolic of the economic and cultural growth that germinated throughout Europe after the end of the Second World War. Yet, visitors to the city will often explore the burnt-out ruins of the old St Michael's Cathedral, bombed to near destruction in the Blitz, without casting an eye to, let alone visiting, its adjacent successor. There is romance in a ruin.

St Felix's Church in Babingley is a wonderful example of this. There isn't a view of it that is unfavourable and, to the most trigger happy of us, nor can a bad photograph be taken of it. The romance is dark and rich. Gazing upon its shell – or, if you are lucky enough to be granted permission to walk in its shadows – wild imaginings stalk you in much the same way a cat hunts a mouse. There are myriad stories to be told here and many more spirits to share their telling.

St Felix was built in the fourteenth century and used for worship for nearly 500 years. Claims abound for it to be recognised as the first Christian church to have been built in Norfolk. These came from the story of St Felix, who was born in Burgundy, arriving at the site by virtue of a shipwreck that cast him upon a shore many miles from his chosen destination. Rescued from drowning by a colony of community-minded beavers, Felix was overcome with gratitude for their help – so much so that, in a state of emotion similar to that which affected the Roman Emperor Caligula so much when he made his horse a senator, Felix duly made one of the beavers a bishop. That act is celebrated to this day on Babingley's village sign, which depicts the grateful St Felix handing a bishop's mitre to the beaver in question, along with instructions to build a church on the site of his rescue.

Naturally enough, the beavers had little to no problem cutting down the trees required, although the fact that they lack opposable thumbs did make its building a little tricky for them. Luckily for both Felix and the beavers, his exploits had come to the attention of the Wuffingas, who, being the East Anglian royal family at the time, invited Felix to spread the word all over their kingdom, as well as providing the labour required to build his church.

Little to nothing remains of the original building now, with the surviving ruin mostly fourteenth-century together with a fifteenth-century porch at the south that is built of brick. Given its ecclesiastical importance both locally and nationally, it's a church that has, sadly, been woefully neglected by successive generations – so much so in fact that its chancel (the part of a church near the altar that is reserved for the clergy and choir) was described as being 'decayed' in a survey of churches that took place in 1602, a description that was amended to 'dilapidated' when a similar survey on the church was carried out in 1752. Photographs taken shortly after the end of the Second World War show St Felix's as still having part of a roof but, as this book's magical photograph of the church as it is today shows (courtesy of Norfolk photographer Nigel Nudds), the building is now entirely roofless and at the complete mercy of the Norfolk elements.

St Felix's Church has been a ruin for some considerable time. You can only wonder how many more generations will be fortunate enough to explore the site and wonder what might have been before it is lost altogether.

Please note that St Felix's Church is on private land and can only be visited with permission given by the landowner.

(Nigel Nudds)

Chapter 4

Baconsthorpe

Castle

A castle always brings out the small boy in me. I want to run along the battlements, shoot pretend arrows out of the arrowslits in the walls and shut the dungeon doors on any fellow visitors who might happen to tarry a-while after I have left their inky depths for a life of light, space and freedom once more. And I'm not the only middle-aged man who feels this way when he visits a castle, because they are adventure playgrounds that knock any and all computer games into a cocked hat. Some are splendid in scale and preservation – Arundel in West Sussex, for example. Others are fairytale-like in sight and setting. Bodiam Castle in neighbouring East Sussex ticks those boxes with its mighty moat acting as a reflection for the multi-turreted behemoth that lurks within it. But fine as they are, they're not 'proper' castles – not in the truest sense, because a proper castle's majesty lays in how weather-beaten and tired it looks.

Take Baconsthorpe Castle, for example. The extensive ruins here are a Pre-Raphaelite's dream come true. For these ancient walls could be the backdrop to romance, revenge and tragedy on a grand scale; indeed, had Tennyson visited this place during its quiet years of decay, then one of his most well-known poems might well have told of the Lady of Baconsthorpe rather than Shalott.

The castle was established by the Heydons, a local well-to-do family, in the fifteenth century. It started its life as the rather more understated Baconsthorpe Hall, but as the family's wealth and power increased, so did the size of their hall until it could fit that description no further and was, to all extents and purposes, a castle – not one that had ever seen a siege or a battle mind, but still a castle. This suited John Heydon, the family member who was responsible for much of the estate's growth. Its size and scale suited him down to the ground for he was an ambitious and successful lawyer as well as an eager social climber who had already changed his family name from Baxton to Heydon in order to disguise their otherwise rather more humble origins as members of the yeomanry. Heydon realised that if he wanted to be rich and powerful then he needed a home that reflected that power as well as his influence on the surrounding lands, much of which he already owned. And, while his living in a hall might have got him some grudging respect, lording it in a castle would not only bring respect, but fear. His policy worked. By the time of his death in 1479, he was both feared and hated across the region. Mission accomplished.

His great work on the main castle was completed by his son, Henry Haydon. Henry was the more retiring type however, and didn't particularly want to live his life as reviled as his father had been. He therefore manipulated his way into London money by way of marriage and became a sheep farmer, restoring, in the process, his family's ancient links with the life and trade of the humble yeoman – a very wealthy one of course, but a yeoman nonetheless. With it he also toned down what he considered to be the more 'in your face' aspects of the castle's character, softening

12

its edges and creating over time a building that was latterly described as more of an 'upmarket courtyard house'.

No doubt his father span in his grave at the very thought of his unyielding stronghold being softened up by his sheep farmer son.

The decline of John Heydon's dream wasn't long in coming, however, and with the near collapse of the wool trade, the Heydons soon found themselves falling into debt that successive generations could only repair by selling off parts of the estate – a long and painful ongoing process that led, ultimately, to the rapidly decaying site being placed in the care of the wartime government in 1940.

Baconsthorpe Castle is now in the very capable hands of English Heritage, an organisation who know a good ruin with a great story when they see one. And Baconsthorpe's is exceptional. It is a symbol of social climbing; of rise, fall and eventual collapse and decay, both literally and figuratively.

(Colin Cubitt)

Chapter 5

Binham

Priory

St Mary's Priory in Binham is a ruined Benedictine Priory that still utilises the nave of a large priory church on the site, which has become the Church of St Mary and the Holy Cross. The surrounding ruins of the priory, as romantic in appearance as any you will find in the country, are now in the tender care of English Heritage, who have made the site freely accessible to all.

The priory was founded in 1091 by Peter de Valognes, a Norman noble who, following the Norman Conquest in 1066, became one of England's wealthiest landowners. He was a man who ended up doing very well out of William the Conqueror's well-planned invasion as, between 1070 and 1076, he was granted lands in Cambridgeshire, Essex, Hertfordshire, Lincolnshire, Norfolk and Suffolk – a considerable haul by any standards. By the time the Domesday Book was completed in 1086, de Valognes had gone on to become sheriff of both Essex and Hertfordshire, eminent titles and privilege enough for two men, let alone one. Yet, for all that, his most valuable land was at Binham, where he eventually settled and married Albreda de Rie, the daughter of Hubert de Rie, the steward of Normandy.

The priory had fairly humble beginnings with only eight monks in situ. This rose to around double that number by the fourteenth century before falling back to just six by the time of the Dissolution of the Monasteries, courtesy of its attendant vandals and thugs paying the priory a visit in 1539.

One of the reasons for such modest monastic beginnings at Binham might have been the considerable time it took to build the priory, estimated to have been around 150 years. This is in stark contrast to building times at some of the world's more recognisable sites, such as the Coliseum in Rome, which took around ten years to build, while the Parthenon above the ancient Greek city of Athens took seventeen years from conception to completion. Indeed, this is an early example of how no-one in Norfolk is in a particular hurry to do anything. An admirable quality.

Because of the great length of time it took to complete the priory, the discerning architect will, upon close inspection of the ruins, notice more than one building style in its weathered walls and arches with both Norman and early English styles visible within the priory church. Following the Dissolution, the building's ruins were given to Sir Thomas Paston who, it seems, wasn't particularly thrilled with his gift – so much so that he ordered most of the buildings to be dismantled. All of them, that is, apart from the fine church, which is still in use today.

Binham is not without its tales and, apocryphal or not, one of the most famous surround the Ley Tunnel (one that follows the course of ancient ley lines) that is said to run from the building's ruins to an unknown site. The story claims that one day a particularly inquisitive fiddler decided to explore these passages, marking his journey as he did so by playing the instrument so that those more sensible folk above the ground could chart his progress. After he had travelled for some considerable distance, the sound of his fiddle suddenly, and without warning, stopped. He was never seen or heard of again.

It is perhaps best to avoid any tunnels in the vicinity then. The ruined priory and church are, however, quite magical and well worth a visit.

(Christine Matthews at Geograph.org.uk)

Chapter 6

Brancaster

Wreck of SS *Vina*

The romance that surrounds the subject of shipwrecks is undeniable. Its place in popular folklore was heightened by the sinking of the RMS *Titanic* in 1912 – a calamitous tale of complacency that led to a seafaring tragedy that had been perceived as impossible. *Titanic* instantaneously became the definitive shipwreck, a byword for loss on an almost incalculable scale. Its place in history was reinforced when its last resting place was finally located in 1985. A smash hit film followed in 1997, and, with it, *Titanic*'s place in popular culture and in the consciousness of anyone who dreams of '... a tall ship and a star to steer her by' was secured forever.

The truth of it is that few people can resist the lure of a shipwreck. This is a fact of life that extends even to the shapeless lumps of rusting iron that lie on a sandbank just off the popular beach at Brancaster. Innocuous they might be, and yet that flame to the imagination that any shipwreck ignites means that this one remains an irresistible magnet to the curious, unwary and, more often than should be the case, the positively foolhardy.

The remains in question are that of the SS *Vina*, a coaster (a shallow-hulled ship used for trade between ports, in this case, sailing a route between those on Britain's east coast and those on the Baltic) that was built by the famous Scottish shipbuilders Ramage & Leith in Leith for J. T. Salvesen & Co. Ltd. Coasters were worked very hard and sailed in predominantly rough seas and unforgiving weather so, when *Vina* was nearing the end of her useful seagoing life in 1940, she was requisitioned by the Royal Navy for wartime use as a blockship (i.e. one that is deliberately sunk in order to prevent the ingress of an aggressive enemy force into a key port or harbour). She was, at the time, one of just three vessels of her type that the owners possessed, the other nine having been lost to enemy U-Boat action. *Vina*'s ultimate fate, therefore, was to be scuttled near the harbour mouth at Great Yarmouth – an action that would have, temporarily at least, delayed any planned Nazi invasion along that part of the coast. With her hold packed with explosives and concrete, *Vina* was towed into position and left there for four years, before, with the threat of invasion abating by the day, she was moved again, this time to the shallow waters off Titchwell (a mile or so to the west of Brancaster), where she was scheduled to be used as target practice for the Allied air forces that would be taking part in the invasion of Normandy on D-Day in 1944.

Yet *Vina*, the great survivor, did not want to die such a violent death. Imbued still with the spirit of the sea and with the salt still running through her iron veins, she slipped from her anchorage during a gale on the night of 19/20 August 1944 and ran. Adrift, she sailed for one final time before running aground in the shallow waters to the west of Scolt Head Island, which is where she resides to this day.

If you take a trip to Brancaster on a hot summer's day in order to enjoy the wide open spaces and skies that this triumph of the Norfolk countryside has to offer, cast a leisurely eye over to

Vina's last resting place and count how many explorers and would-be treasure hunters you can see picking over her remains. On some days the crowds of people gathered out there would be more befitting to Stonehenge rather than *Vina*'s much more recent remains, of which her triple expansion engine is perhaps the most identifiable part. She is hardly treasure and hardly, as it stands, a sight worth losing your life for. Powerful currents run between the wreck and the beach and there have been instances of unwary sightseers drowning after walking out to take a closer look only to find themselves cut off by the incoming tide.

Although she provides a striking image against the Norfolk skies and is a wreck that, just like any other, has a fascinating story to tell, it is best in this instance to observe from a safe distance.

(Julian Dowse at Geograph.org.uk)

Chapter 7

Brancaster Staithe

RAF Barrow Common

Barrow Common is a large and undulating area of predominantly acidic grassland, a wonderful mix of gorse, bracken and other native species that inhabit its gentle folds, which include a disused sandpit, some woodland and ancient chalk workings.

It is a wonderful place to take yourself for a quiet hour or two, and the emphasis here really is on 'quiet'. Even on the sunniest and most idyllic of summer weekends, Barrow Common will only have a small scattering of cars dotted about the road edges, so a walk here can, over even an hour, hour and a half or more, see you encounter no more than one or two other people plus an occasional overfriendly dog. It is a time-worn site (the word 'barrow' is Germanic in origin and refers to a mound of earth and stones raised over a grave or network of graves) that is, in my opinion, best visited at twilight at the end of a long, hot June day when the shadows are falling across the gorse and the birds have gone to their roosts in the rich woodland areas that bound the common. These are trees bent and gnarled with age; sentinels for this most beguiling of places where, in the shadows, your imagination can quite easily run away with thoughts of a more ancient time when the harebell, meadowsweet and lady's bedstraw might have been part of a more menacing landscape than the one we can all enjoy today.

Barrow Common has been the site of man's darker inclinations in modern times as well as ancient ones. It dwells, certainly for this part of the world, at a more than handsome height above sea level and boasts a clear view over the surrounding landscape, salt marsh and sea, including, when the tide is out, a fine view of our old friend the SS *Vina* (see 6) marooned on her lonely sandbank. This lofty perch and the wide open vista of sky, sea and land it gave from west to east prompted the Ministry of Defence to use it as the site for RAF Barrow Common, a Chain Home Low (CHL) radar station which was used to detect aircraft flying at altitudes that the more 'traditional' stations could not detect (i.e. those that were flying as low as 500 feet).

RAF Barrow Common was brought into service in 1940 and for the first two years of its operational life was manned by members of the army before switching to joint Royal Navy and RAF use with the Royal Navy being given the task of tracking and identifying the vast array of ships that could be seen travelling the long stretch of coast in the distance. Four members of Royal Navy personnel would be on active duty at any one time, although the total number of men stationed at RAF Barrow Common totalled nearer to eighty at the peak of its active use. They would not, however, all have been at the station at the same time and would, for the most part, have been billeted at a barn in nearby Brancaster Staithe.

The ruins of RAF Barrow Common consist of two main buildings, the larger of which was used as the main operations block. Internally, this was divided into three separate rooms, the most westerly of which could have held some radar equipment that was positioned on top of a concrete plinth. Of these three rooms, an interesting feature in the middle one is the site of numerous cabling channels in the floor, which would have been used to hold the vast amount of electrical cable that would have been needed to bring adequate power to the site and its equipment, the most notable component of which was the radar aerial itself. This was originally positioned on the roof of the operations block, evidence of which can be seen today in the iron holding bolts that are still visible on the roof. The aerial, which was around 200 feet high, was later moved to a new site some 100 yards to the south-east of the main buildings.

RAF Barrow Common is clearly visible and accessible today, although you can no longer enter the buildings, which are managed by the Barrow Common Management Committee.

(Ken Tidd)

Chapter 8

Briningham

Bellevue Tower

'Rapunzel, Rapunzel, let down your hair ...' The words from that famous Grimm fairytale came to me in an instant when I first cast my eyes over the vision that is the Bellevue Tower at Briningham, a quiet village that lies around 20 miles north-west of Norwich. It stands, alone and proud, against Norfolk's massive skies, inviting tales of mystery. This is a structure you cannot 'just' take in once for, as you survey the view, your eyes demand, again and again, to be drawn back to it, to look again and move just a little closer. As you do so, thoughts abound and you wonder will, in the merest twinkling of an eye, this fairytale tower suddenly be gone again, returned to the mystical realm from whence it came? Fortunately not, for most assuredly, Bellevue Tower is very much a part of Norfolk's landscape as well as its history.

It was built as a smock mill – a windmill that consists of a sloping, horizontally weatherboarded or thatched tower that usually has either six or eight sides. The tower is then topped off with a roof cap that rotates so that the sails can be brought into the wind. The name 'smock' mill derives from that form of dress that farmers wore in the seventeenth and eighteenth centuries as the mill's shape supposedly resembles a farmer clad in his favourite piece of daywear.

Briningham Smock Mill was built by the 1st Baronet of Melton Constable Hall, Sir Jacob Astley, in 1721. It wasn't, however, one of either his or his builders' finest creations and was replaced around fifty years later by a more reliable and up to date three-storey brick tower topped off with a cupola (a tall, dome-like structure) roof that sat atop a new roof, which was castellated in order to give it the appearance of the battlements on a castle.

Its days of working life were soon numbered and it was converted into everyday residential use towards the end of the eighteenth century, the first windmill in Norfolk to suffer from this inglorious fate. In doing so, it became something of an extravagant folly known, as it is today, as the Belle Vue Tower, the name 'Belle Vue' translating from French into 'nice view' – a description that no-one can really argue with. It was one that was described by a Mr Arthur Young in his compelling tome *The Farmers Tour Through The East Of England* (1771) as '... a prodigious view of a rich woodland country, fully intermixed with cornfields and wanting nothing but a river to be complete'. Clearly, Mr Young had very exacting standards when it came to views and probably thought the 315-foot-high spire at Norwich Cathedral was 'too pointy'. The view from the top of Belle Vue Tower is today, much to his disappointment you would suspect, much the same; there is still no river of course, but plentiful evidence of woodland and good agricultural land with views of up to 20–25 miles distant

The tower has had some more practical applications. It was used, for example, as a lookout point by the local Home Guard during the Second World War, when its owner at the time, Lord Hastings (Lieutenant Colonel Lord Hastings at that), would rally the local platoon at its base and order them to spend long and somewhat lonely days and nights at its peak keeping an eye out for invading Nazi hoards. More truthfully, they were just seeing who was about and what they were bally well up to, especially if it came to a spot of poaching on his Lordship's land. How handy it must have been to have a 60-foot-high tower on land that was, at over 300 feet above sea level, positively mountainous for Norfolk!

Belle Vue Tower was extensively renovated from the mid-1970s into the 1980s and beyond and is now a private residence.

(Ray Blyth)

Chapter 9

Brograve

Level Drainage Mill

A little story to start things off here. When I was ten, Brancaster Primary School took a group of us to the How Hill Education Centre near the village of Ludham in the Norfolk Broads. It was a two-night residential stay – one that was, for many of us, the very first time we had ever been away from home.

I have many memories of that stay but the most vivid remains that of an old ruined windmill on the banks of the River Ant that was in sight of the main house and gardens. It was one that transfixed and beguiled me for the whole of my stay there, a sight I could never let go of and one I forever found myself drawn to whenever the opportunity presented itself.

I now find that the ruin of the Brograve Level Drainage Mill has a similar effect. It is equally, in my eyes, as majestic yet sepulchral as that of the windmill that so embraced the imagination of my childhood, stark and forbidding on the banks of the Ant. Brograve looks like the sort of mill that Don Quixote would have tilted at. He would have lost. For, even in its twenty-first-century desolation, this windmill remains mighty.

You can find it on the Brograve Level within the parish of Sea Palling, around 1 mile north of Horsey Mere. It was built by Sir Berny Brograve in 1771 in order to drain the rapidly encroaching waters from his surrounding land. Sir Berny was, by all accounts, a bit of a local character, so much so in fact that he hid in the mill after a disagreement with the devil one night. According to legend, the devil pounded his hooves on the door in an attempt to get in throughout the night but was unable to gain entry (respect is due here, I feel, to whoever made the door in question), although Sir Berny could not help but notice as he left the next morning that the door was now covered in hoof prints.

Whether or not there are any physical marks remaining in and around the windmill that further pay attest to Sir Berny's nocturnal visitor I will leave for the curious explorer to conclude as they make their own observations of the site from the safety of the opposite bank. But it would be best, perhaps, to do so in the daytime, wouldn't you think?

The mill, when it wasn't being used as a hiding place, operated and was powered by an internal turbine that operated its four sails, draining in the process the waters from the Brograve Levels into a small river known as the Waxham New Cut – a day-to-day obligation that the mill faithfully met until it finally succumbed to old age in 1930 and ceased working.

Of those four original sails, the stubs of two remain in place, sculptural against the sky and still, for all their weathered state, an impressive sight to see as well as a remarkable feat of engineering given the scale of the whole operation. Brograve Mill cannot now be directly accessed by foot so the only feasible way of getting to it would be by water, an altogether ill-advised method for all but the most experienced of those who sail upon the dark and forbidding waters of the Norfolk Broads.

It is much better then to observe it from the path that winds along the Waxham New Cut from the nearby Horsey Mere. And perhaps viewing this behemoth from another time from a distance is the best way to do so for the whole structure, including the heavy mill machinery that dwells within, is now completely open to the elements and is, as a result, becoming increasingly unsafe to enter.

Sadly, the day may not be too far off when Brograve is a pile of undistinguished rubble, with perhaps, if we are lucky, a sign informing people of her past glories.

(Carmina McConnell at Shutterstock.com)

Chapter 10

Castle Acre

Castle

I wonder how many people who grew up in Norfolk in the 1970s and 1980s can remember their Sunday roast being enlivened by the promise that lunch would be followed by a 'little ride out to Castle Acre' that same afternoon?

There aren't many villages in Norfolk that offer such an impressive entrance and first impression as the Bailey Gate, the stentorian guardian of the village. It was one of two such gatehouses that were added to the original settlement's earthwork defences and dates from around 1200. Sadly, little is known of the other gatehouse, which has only ever yielded information about its existence from an observation made about it in the eighteenth century. Thankfully, the Bailey Gate has survived to tell many a tale and will quite likely do so for many more centuries to come. It consists of a pointed archway that is flanked by solid semi-circular turrets, behind which the passage that led to the interior of the old settlement could be protected from undesirables with a gate and portcullis.

Walking or driving through it today, you can only be impressed by its sheer physical presence and the impact it must have made upon generation after generation of people who have lived, worked in or visited the village. It is as significant and impressive a sight today as it ever was, particularly in this time of ugly and ill-fitting buildings that lack soul and are built with profit rather than purpose in mind.

As for the village of Castle Acre itself, prepare to have to sit down in order to fully take in and appreciate its amazing history. It is, for one, a rare and complete example of a Norman planned settlement which, apart from the castle itself, includes much of the present-day village, its parish church and, in Castle Acre Priory, one of the best preserved monastic sites in the whole country.

These sites were all the work of the Warennes, a great Norman baronial family who made their indelible impact upon Castle Acre throughout the eleventh and twelfth centuries. The castle itself was founded shortly after the Battle of Hastings by William de Warenne (the family name originated in the French village of Varenne in Normandy), who was a close friend of none other than William the Conqueror – a great position to find yourself in if you are allied to the victor but not such a good one if you are on the losing side. Fortunately for William de Warenne, he sided with a serial winner.

His castle reflects the strength and majesty of England's new champion, a well-preserved and visually stunning example of a motte and bailey castle – that is, a fortification that has a stone keep built upon a raised defensive earthwork, the motte, which is in turn encompassed by an enclosed courtyard, namely the bailey. One of the original gatehouses to the latter remains *in situ* today, the afore mentioned Bailey Gate.

You can be forgiven, of course, if you thought it was named after a Mr Bailey, but it's not that ridiculous a notion. One of the origins for the name 'Bailey' is from the old French 'baillis' or 'bailif' as well as the middle English 'bail' and can refer, in all instances, to someone whose role in life was an official of some kind; a steward for example, or possibly a gatekeeper. So there may well have been a bailey within the Bailey Gate named after its purpose rather than after a particular person.

Fascinating little possibilities at a fascinating site that is well worth a visit and, at the very least, the post Sunday afternoon visit I mentioned earlier on. Castle Acre is currently in the safe and expert stewardship of English Heritage – who, I suspect, may have more than their fair share of Baileys in their august ranks.

(Ray Blyth)

Chapter 11

Covehithe

St Andrew's Church

This must have been a magnificent church in its time. The ruins of St Andrew's Church at Covehithe remind me of the equally dramatic St Margaret's Church in Cley next the Sea on the Norfolk coast. Had it stood in one of Europe's great cities – Florence for example, or Paris or Rome – I am convinced it would be as much a part of the 'must see' sights for those places as any other that they may contain. Yet, there it sits, alone and exposed in a small Norfolk village, a carelessly misplaced cathedral in splendid isolation – its derelict north and south transepts a sign of how prohibitively expensive a large church was for a small community.

Because the grim reality was that if any church started to fall into a state of disrepair and its tiny band of worshippers had no means by which they could afford the necessary reparations, then things were just left to get steadily worse and worse until only ruins stood where there had once been walls and worship. St Margaret's is a little battered about the edges, but she has prevailed. Sadly for the grandiose church that once stood in equal majesty in Covehithe, St Andrew's would, ultimately, meet a much more unfortunate fate.

The dereliction of St Andrew's dates from 1672, which was barely 200 years after she was first built. This did not solely come about through violence or riot, nor discontent or dissolution. Its fall to rack and ruin was simply down to the fact that the continuing financial upkeep of such a great church was too much for a tiny village to manage, especially at a time when public worship was regarded as being more about quiet devotion and public modesty rather than ostentatious displays of wealth and power.

A desperate parish made it clear that it could not afford to manage such a lavish building. Their pleas were heard and they were given permission to remove its roof and build a much smaller and more humble church in place of the gargantuan original. It nestles, suitably meek and mild, within the ruins today, the only remnants of its predecessor being the lofty tower and some of the vast original walling.

Covehithe was not totally exempt from deliberate vandalism, however. Before the roof was finally and irrevocably removed, St Andrew's was paid a visit by a William Dowsing. He was, as far as medieval churches were concerned, as much a nemesis as Richard Beeching was later to become for the region's railways. Dowsing was a fervent Puritan and iconoclast; that is, one who holds the social belief that it was vitally important to destroy religious icons, statues, monuments and other images. St Andrew's, with around 200 such images beautifully created and revered in its stained glass, didn't stand a chance against his destructive leanings. He would, furthermore, have been given every encouragement and assistance in destroying them by the Churchwardens of St Andrew's, who would undoubtedly have been Puritans themselves.

The present-day ruins are under the care of the Churches Conservation Trust. Their cause and work in preserving such sites is to be admired, but even they will not be able to prevent the ultimate fate of the site, which will one day fall prey to the North Sea as ongoing erosion steadily and inevitably wears away at the nearby coastal fringes. As a result, one day Covehithe will be as much a legend as the church at nearby Dunwich.

(BMA at Shutterstock.com)

Chapter 12

Docking

RAF Docking

Norfolk almost became the fifty-first State of America during the Second World War. The reason for this was the huge number of US airbases and their personnel that were dotted all over the county from the early 1940s onwards. Some of these airfields became quite well known, RAF Coltishall and RAF Sculthorpe being two examples, the latter being particularly famous for its surviving (of three) runway. At 9,000 feet in length, it's one of the longest in Europe and, despite the fact that the base 'officially' closed in the early 1990s, said runway remains in operational use to this day because, according to local legend, RAF Sculthorpe had been designated as one of several emergency landing sites for the Space Shuttle as well as other (unnamed) aircraft. A rural myth, surely? I contacted NASA to ask them for their thoughts on the matter and, after a long delay, got a reply which, in essence, claimed that '…we can neither confirm nor deny this'. So the story is true then. Interesting.

The skies in this part of Norfolk were certainly very busy from the 1940s onwards. RAF Docking, which began its life as a decoy site that displayed dummy aircraft and infrastructure, was intended to convince the enemy it was an operational airfield when it was not. Eventually, it became more functionally operational when it assumed a role as a satellite airfield for nearby RAF Bircham Newton in July 1940. This meant that, for whatever reasons, aircraft that could not be accommodated at Bircham Newton would divert to Docking and land there. RAF Docking eventually got its own squadron, namely No. 235 Squadron RAF, who used the formidable Bristol Blenheim aircraft for convoy escort and anti-shipping operations in the North Sea.

The base had eight blister hangars, which were portable and made of steel or wooden ribs and usually covered with steel sheets, plus one A1 (permanent) hangar. A meteorological unit, No. 1401 (Met) Flight, was soon seconded to Docking, which meant that far from being a quiet and somewhat provincial offshoot of RAF Bircham Newton (as would have been the initial intention), Docking became more and more actively involved with the war effort and ultimately saw a very great variety of aircraft making regular visits to the site; for example, Hurricanes, Spitfires and Gloster Gladiator biplanes. Eventually, No. 1401 (Met) Flight was made into a squadron in its own right. Named No. 521 Squadron, it included Lockheed Hudson and Hampden aircraft as well as one of the most famous twin-engine multirole aircraft that was ever conceived and built, namely the de Havilland Mosquito. This iconic wooden aircraft would head out of Docking and towards the North Sea at Brancaster, from where they would operate deep into occupied Europe in order to take measurements over potential target areas for RAF Bomber Command.

RAF Docking's close proximity to the coast meant that it was also pressed into use for emergency landings by aircraft that were returning from missions over continental Europe. Unlike those at RAF Sculthorpe, however, Docking's runways were short and stories abounded about one lucky USAAF pilot who touched down his B17 Flying Fortress bomber halfway along the runway, still carrying a full bomb load, and ended up crashing through a hedge into an adjacent field.

So make no mistake about it, RAF Docking was no rural backwater. It played a full and important role in the Second World War and should most certainly be recognised for having done so. Except that it isn't, which is a great pity. This situation was at least partially readdressed in 2007 when a memorial was erected on the grass verge where a small copse hides some of the sites few remaining buildings. It can be seen as you drive north into Brancaster along the B1153 road from Docking itself. Fitting and appropriate.

(Richard Humphrey at Geograph.org.uk)

Chapter 13

East Somerton

St Mary's Church

If you want a touch of drama mixed into your landscape – an otherwise pleasant but peaceful walk interrupted by a moment of adrenaline-induced shock – then this is the place to come.

The ruins of St Mary's Church in East Somerton are set half a mile or so down a woodland track in the grounds of Burnley Hall, but don't expect to find them that easily. Indeed, you should be far more prepared for the church to find *you,* for so absorbed will you be in the majesty of the woodland canopy and the massive beech and oak trees that contribute to it, you won't really know that you have located the ruins until you are well and truly in it. Suddenly you are there, in the midst of what would have been an enormous church; one that has, over time, blended in with its surroundings and given what is left of its great nave and tower to nature and made ivy and elder its adornments rather than stained glass and iconic images.

It can feel as if this is a building that will eat you alive, for as you stand before the chancel arch with its overgrown backdrop, you could be about to step into a mighty ecclesiastical maw. Ruined this church may be, lost and largely forgotten it most certainly is, but do not doubt the power it still wields over both its lush surrounds and the (usually) unwary visitor.

The demise of St Mary's came about when the Parish of East Somerton was stripped of its own identity and assumed into that of neighbouring Winterton-on-Sea and its impressive Church of the Holy Trinity and All Saints. St Mary's remained in use as a chapel for the use of the family and workers at Burnley Hall but its physical fate had already been sealed for, as with the great church at Covehithe (see 15), it became more and more impractical and, eventually, impossible for a such a small community to adequately be able to support such a large church.

Legend abounds that a witch with a wooden leg was buried in the nave of the church and that the giant oak tree which now soars into the heavens from the ruins of the nave is the spirit of that witch who, over time, has assumed the form of a tree that has contributed to the destruction of St Mary's.

A tale which one might find easy to dismiss as country folklore and the sort of story that is told over a foaming pint in the warmth and safety of a local pub on winter evenings? Maybe. But would you trust your nerves enough to spend some time alone amidst the ruins of St Mary's in the twilight and wait for the shadows to overtake you until darkness falls at this extraordinary site? You're a braver soul than I am if that is indeed the case.

(Colin Cubitt)

Chapter 14

Elveden

War Memorial

This commanding war memorial that sits adjacent to the busy A11 is neither a traditional ruin nor a folly but still justifies its inclusion in this book as a reminder to us all of the folly of war.

At 127 feet in height it is one of the tallest war memorials in Britain as well as being one of the most striking. It was commissioned by the Earl of Iveagh to commemorate the forty-eight men from Elveden and the adjacent parishes of Icklingham and Enswell who lost their lives in the First World War. Fittingly, it stands on a spot where those three parishes meet.

The aftermath of that terrible conflict saw a massive wave of public commemoration sweep over the nation with, in England alone, tens of thousands of memorials being erected as countless communities, large and small, tried to come to terms with not only the loss of around 750,000 British lives, but the official policy at the time of not repatriating the dead. This meant that the memorials became the main focus of those communities' grief and a place where, to this day, poppy wreathes are laid every Remembrance Sunday.

The Elveden estate where the memorial stands had belonged to Edward Cecil Guinness, a noted philanthropist who had, in 1919, been created Earl of Iveagh and Viscount Elveden. He commissioned the monument from Clyde Young, son of William, who had, towards the end of the nineteenth century, been the mastermind behind an extension to Elveden Hall that had included a new east wing.

The memorial's costs were met by Guinness, although it should be said that he invited parishioners to contribute to the costs if they wished, something many of them did. Guinness is said to have been partially motivated, with regard to the design and impact on the landscape that the memorial has, by the monument to Coke of Norfolk at Holkham Hall (see 23), requesting that this memorial be taller than the one dedicated to Coke but not as tall as Nelson's Column in Trafalgar Square. For the record, the Elveden Memorial, at 127 feet, is 4 feet higher than its contemporary in Holkham but still nearly 20 feet shorter than Nelson's Column.

Elveden War Memorial is a Corinthian column made of Weldon stone that is surmounted by an urn made of Portland stone. It is a Grade II* listed building that is protected and listed on the National Heritage List for England that is maintained by Historic England. It is a fitting memorial to a lost generation.

(Stephen McKay at Geograph.org.uk)

Chapter 15

Eye

Crinkle Crankle Wall

A wall? Yes indeed. Even the humble wall (the one that surrounds the great house and estate at Holkham Hall in Norfolk is so long, my late father used to insist whenever we passed it, that it could be seen from space) can be, to steal a popular expression from twenty-first-century youth, 'pimped' up. Pimp my wall as it were.

A crinkle crankle wall can, surprisingly, save money for the creative builder behind their construction because they can be made with the thickness of just one brick, a money-saving technique that will only work if the wall is given a sinuous configuration as the alternate convex (curving outwards) and concave (curving inwards) design provides stability, helping the entire body of the wall resist any exterior forces pushing against it. It is ironic, therefore, that a construction method designed to save on man hours, material and money is still regarded as being excessive when the reality is that it is anything but.

The term 'crinkle crankle' is believed to be an old English phrase meaning to zig-zag, with the phrase really coming into vogue during the eighteenth century, when it was applied to the many walls of that type that were appearing all over the country as the trend caught on with the owners of large country homes and estates.

Yet these walls did not come into existence because they were considered some sort of wavy status symbol. Far from it. For, as well as bringing about the economic benefits already mentioned, they also had a practical application; if, as was the practice, a garden wall was aligned east–west, the side that was facing south would catch the warming rays of the sun and be ideal as a location for the growing of fruit.

Crinkle crankle walls are found throughout East Anglia, their presence down to the presence of Dutch engineers (the most famous of which was Sir Cornelius Vermuyden) who, when they were not being kept busy draining the marshes of the Fens, amused themselves by building walls which they referred to as 'slangenmuur', which translated from Dutch means 'snake wall'.

Eye's famous crinkle crankle wall surrounds the main house and grounds of Chandos Lodge, believed to have been built and named after Anna Eliza, the then Duchess of Chandos, who died in 1813. It seems fitting that an unusual wall borders the home that is named after her, for she herself seems to have lived a life that weaved a wavy path of its own, full of ups and downs. She made her way through three husbands, bearing three daughters to her second husband, one of whom was given the catchy and easy to remember name of Lady Anne Elizabeth Nugent-Temple-Brydges-Chandos-Grenville.

The Duchess's second husband, James Brydges, 3rd Duke of Chandos, suffered a somewhat unfortunate fate when he died after Anna Eliza pulled a chair out from under him, an incident that led to her suffering from mental health problems – so much so in fact that, in 1791, a court decreed that she was a lunatic whose daughters had to be placed in the care of guardians.

Another previous owner of the house and wall was Frederick Ashton, the founding choreographer of the Royal Ballet. You suspect he would have found the graceful leanings of his garden wall particularly pleasing.

It should be noted that Chandos Lodge and its grounds are not open to the public. There is, however, nothing to stop you admiring the fine lines of its crinkle crankle wall from the outside.

(Ray Blyth)

Chapter 16

Freston

Freston Tower

I have, freely and admittedly, been a little bit fast and loose with what exactly constitutes a folly in this book. For me, it is a term that can be applied to any building or structure that goes beyond that line in the sand that marks off where conformity ends and visual rebellion begins. Thus a water tower need not look like a castle, nor need a five-storey tower be built when a two-storey house would meet the owners' needs in exactly the same manner. And neither does any house need an orangery when it can have a greenhouse. An orangery does, of course, at least have a practical purpose whereas, traditionally, a folly need not. Yet they are hardly necessary and can be considered, in all cases, an indulgence – especially in the more remote parts of Norfolk, and especially orangeries built in locations that are on the same line of latitude* as the Strait of Tartary in Russia, Semisopochnoi Island in Alaska and Saskatchewan in Canada.

Where Freston Tower is concerned, however, I don't think anyone can argue that it isn't a folly, or, come to that, the very definition of one. It could be the example sitting next to the word in any reputable dictionary.

It's reputed to be the oldest folly in England, with its construction reckoned to have taken place as far back as sometime in the fifteenth century. This is supported by the claim that the tower was commissioned and built by a Lord de Freston for the exclusive use of his daughter, with each of the six floors dedicated to a different area of learning, meaning that, from Monday through to Saturday, she studied a certain subject on each of the tower's floors. Fittingly, the top floor was reserved to astronomy, complete with all of the latest scientific instruments which she could use to take and record her observations.

As appealing as this story is, it is alas also apocryphal as it forms part of the plot of a novel written by the Reverend Richard Cobbold – clearly, it would seem, a man with rather too much free time on his hands if he could afford to spend it writing fanciful stories rather than tending to his flock, of whom he recorded, in no little detail, lengthy written accounts about them and their day-to-day lives.

What is more likely is that Freston Tower was built in the middle of the seventeenth century to serve as a lookout over the Freston Reach of the River Orwell and that, just like its contemporary in B400ingham, it was being used as a highly visible means of observing the local populace to ensure that they were behaving themselves. It might even have been the case that, on occasion, no watcher from the skies was even needed to be on station at the top of Freston Tower and that its mere presence on the landscape, a real life Barad-dûr (the tower from which Tolkien's Dark Lord watched over his lands in the *Lord of the Rings* trilogy), was enough to persuade most of the locals to toe the line, such was their fear of being observed in the act of poaching or similar.

Such a distinctive and well regarded structure could not, however, have a nefarious purpose in life for too long and by 1730 Freston Tower was available to let, complete with furniture, for anyone who felt like a long weekend in rural Norfolk, an early example if ever there was one of a holiday home with a view.

Towards the end of the eighteenth century it was pressed into use for smallpox patients, its height and relative isolation thought, no doubt, to be as good a reason as any to send the poor individuals there. You can follow in their wretched footsteps to this day should you feel like it as Freston Tower is now owned by the Landmark Trust who let it out, complete with its twenty-six windows and stunning views, as a holiday property. Having smallpox, I should add, is not a requirement for making your booking.

*Blickling sits on a latitude of 52 degrees north – the same as the other locations mentioned.

(Stephen Bashford at Geograph.org.uk)

Chapter 17

Hadleigh

Hadleigh Castle

It's not unknown for someone to buy a house and, within weeks of getting the keys, tear apart any and all vestiges of the previous owners. Kitchen? Rip it all out and start again. Bathroom? Same again. Carpets up, walls repainted different colours, loft converted and treasured lawn turned into a vegetable patch. Not so much keeping up with the Joneses as removing any last traces of them and the home they'd made. This isn't a new phenomenon. The owners of castles did it as well.

The ruins of Hadleigh Castle stand on the fringes of the Thames Estuary to the south of the Essex town from which it takes its name. The castle was built in the early part of the thirteenth century by a Hubert de Burgh who had served as Justiciar (a role not unlike the present one of Prime Minister) under King John, of Magna Carta fame. He was a formidable and influential man then, and one who had powerful friends; a man who felt his standing in life deserved, at the very least, a castle to call his own. He was given the licence to build one by King John, who had in 1230 also gifted him the land it was to stand upon. Such was the size of de Burgh's ego that his castle had by that time already been completed, meaning that the consent given to him by his monarch to do so ended up being retrospective. Luckily for de Burgh, the king and his court were sympathetic to his sense of self-importance and, quite literally, let the matter stand. Try building a castle today without planning permission and see what happens.

However well de Burgh got on with King John, however, he was never going to have the same cosy relationship with King Henry III. The two men rapidly fell out and, in a subsequent act of lordly pique, Henry stripped de Burgh of his ownership of Hadleigh Castle, declaring that it and the lands it stood upon now belonged to the crown. Like rather too many landlords with a property portfolio that they can't keep up with, however, Henry then proceeded to pay scant regard to his new trinket, a surprising decision really, given that Hadleigh was near enough to London to be an ideal weekend retreat, one with great views over the water at that.

It was Edward III who first fully came to recognise Hadleigh's potential when he came to the throne in 1327, a hundred years or so after its initial construction had been completed. And, to him, while the castle had a lot going for it geographically and strategically, its look and decor were, well, to put it bluntly, *so* thirteenth century. So he promptly got the builders in, their remit being to not only make it 'fit for a King' (which would have meant the end of the avocado privy) but bigger and more fit for purpose. This meant it needed to become a fortification that would easily see off a potential attack from the dreaded French but also one grand enough to provide him with (and at last the groat has dropped) with a convenient second home close to London.

Like any petulant teenager, Richard II, Edward's grandson, reckoned that if grandad saw Hadleigh as a good place to visit and spend time in, then it must have been a *really* boring place and certainly not somewhere he wanted to take his friends. So he neglected it completely, meaning that Hadleigh eventually found its way back to the de Burgh family when it was granted to Aubrey in the late fourteenth century. Subsequent owners included Edmund of Langley and his son Edward of Norwich, assorted Dukes of York and a Duke of Gloucester as well as forming part of the dowry granted by King Henry VIII to three of his wives: Catherine of Aragon, Anne of Cleves and Catherine Parr. Henry further made full use of the woodlands surrounding the castle to provide woodland for his rapidly expanding navy. Another owner of Hadleigh Castle was William Booth, the founder of the Salvation Army, who acquired it in 1891 for the use of his organisation, and its current owners are English Heritage. During the 2012 Summer Olympic Games, Hadleigh Park was used as the venue for the mountain biking competition, with the winner of the Women's Cross Country event being Julie Bresset from France. Edward III would have been turning in his grave.

(Diana Mower at Shutterstock.com)

Chapter 18

Hainford

All Saints Church

Hainford's 'new' All Saints Church has the look of one of those lonely little churches you might happen to come across on a rocky hillside while exploring the Mediterranean coast. It was built by the Victorians and superseded the old medieval church of the same name, which was partially demolished in 1840 while the new church was being built.

The west tower still stands to this day. An atmospheric reminder of the onetime place of worship, it is a familiar landmark to those travelling on the adjacent road to Hoveton – yet one, I suspect, that is little more than an image in the corner of their eye to most as they pass. Of the rest of the church, the nave, chancel and south porch are all long gone, although the stones that made them will live on in other buildings close to the old church as the Victorians were as keen on recycling as we are, if not more so, and will have seen to their further use elsewhere.

A great example of this occurred at Brancaster Staithe on the north-west Norfolk coast where a mighty malt house, reputed to be the biggest in the country at the time, was built to store all of the grain that was brought ashore at the port. Naturally enough, such a building needed a lot of raw material to get it, quite literally, off the ground, so you can imagine the builders' delight when they sourced and helped themselves to a large supply of stone found in a field to the east of the neighbouring village of Brancaster. Unfortunately, these stones made up the walls and features of Branodunum, the Roman fort that was built in the village in the early decades of the third century, which had stood, unmoved and, for the most part, unheralded for well over 1,500 years until they met their untimely fate at the hands of overzealous Victorians with their minds rather more focused on profit than history*.

Such was the case at Hainford. The old All Saints Church came down with little or no regard to its importance and value to the community or its historical significance. Its fate was sealed by the Church of England's desire to fight back against the Oxford Movement and its leanings towards Roman Catholicism. This led to the Diocese at Norwich deciding that it needed to make many of its locations of worship more visible and easily reachable for congregations meaning, theoretically, any tendency to drift away from the Church of England would be nullified.

The new Church of All Saints was just such an example – a simple but cost effective and easy to maintain building in a new location that was built in the centre of the village a good half a mile away from the now abandoned original.

Yet the old church site did not fall into immediate disuse, for a nineteenth-century chapel was then built onto the eastern-facing wall of the old tower – a structure that came after the building of the new church. A sign of guilt perhaps, or a sudden reluctance to let go of what was and yield completely to the new? No. This was an entirely practical decision taken when it was realised that the height of the water table in the grounds of the new church in the centre of Hainford would mean it was not suitable for burials and subsequent use as a graveyard. The old site was, and continues be, used for this purpose with the aforementioned chapel (which is now in disuse itself) having been built to allow for a resting place for coffins prior to their being interred in the shadow of the ruined tower.

*Victorian visitors to Stonehenge were given a hammer and chisel upon arrival at the sacred site and invited to hack away at the stones in order to provide themselves with a souvenir of their visit.

(Colin Cubitt)

Chapter 19

Harwich

Wreck of *Terukuni Maru*

Unlike the other sites in this book, the ruins of the *Terukuni Maru* are neither accessible nor easily visible. But it deserves its place as, uniquely, the only casualty to have been suffered by the Japanese Imperial Navy outside of East Asia prior to its attack on Pearl Harbour in 1941.

The *Terukuni Maru* was a Japanese ocean liner owned by the massive Nippon Yusen Kaisha, one of the oldest (it was founded in 1885) and largest shipping companies in the world. She was built by the Mitsubishi Shipbuilding & Engineering Company in Nagasaki and entered service in 1930. At a time when taking a luxury cruise was still seen as the very epitome of personal indulgence, *Terukuni Maru* had been built with little expense spared. Both she and her sister ship, the *Yasukuni Maru,* were intended for the shipping company's high-speed European service, but had been designed with all the rigours of tropical conditions in mind, with state-of-the-art air conditioning and fresh air circulating systems installed throughout. She weighed 11,931 tons and was 505 feet long with a single funnel and two masts. Accommodation onboard allowed for 121 passengers in first class, sixty-eight in second class and sixty in third class with a crew of 177. Her sailing route was intended to be south from Japan and through the Indian Ocean and Suez Canal before heading into the Mediterranean, where all of her passengers, from the extremely rich to the merely considerably well off, would enjoy all that the fancy resorts of the time would have to offer.

This then begs the question as to why she ended up sinking in the cold and muddy waters of the Thames Estuary, within sight of the less than fancy port of Harwich. In truth, there was nothing particularly unusual about the route that she took on her twenty-fifth, and final, voyage to Europe. The circumstances that surround her eventual demise are, however, extremely mysterious and suggest dark goings on and cover ups at the highest levels.

She had departed Yokohama as planned on 24 September 1939, en route to Europe via, among other places, Nagoya, Kobe, Hong Kong, Singapore and Penang. She then made an uneventful crossing of the Suez Canal before visiting Beirut, Naples and Marseilles with the intention of making London her final port of call by mid-November.

While cruising off the South Downs, *Terukuni Maru* took aboard a pilot in order to undergo the usual inspection for contraband while, at the same time, Royal Navy minesweepers checked her route into London, declaring, after a short time, that the way ahead was clear and that the ship could safely proceed into London. This was routine stuff that the Royal Navy would have carried out for visiting ships (Britain and her allies would not declare war on Japan for another two years) on countless occasions without incident or cause for alarm. Until now, at least, for shortly after midnight on the morning of 21 November, and while sailing off the Essex coast, *Terukuni Maru* struck a magnetic mine and sank in under an hour. Fortunately, there were no fatalities and all the passengers and crew onboard at the time were able to escape in lifeboats. But there were more serious consequences to come for, as a neutral nation at the time of the sinking, a diplomatic incident of considerable proportions arose between Japan and both Germany and Great Britain. Each nation denied, vehemently, any involvement in the sinking and went on to accuse their opponent of laying the mine in question. This did not stop the Japanese Government seeking reparations from Nazi Germany but, even though the two nations were natural (and future) allies, no offer of financial recompense or admission of culpability was made by Nazi Germany or, for that matter, the British Government.

The wreckage of *Terukuni Maru* lay under just 50 feet of water and was, for a while, visible to passing shipping. In 1946 she was demolished with explosives as part of a British effort to remove any and all war debris from shallow coastal waters. What remains of her today can be visited by intrepid divers looking to explore the remnants of this once opulent ocean liner – one whose loss might, in the politics of war, have been rather more by design than accident.

(Public Domain)

Chapter 20

Heacham

Scond World War Pillbox

This lonely Second World War pillbox at Heacham is nothing more than a decaying curiosity now; a playground for small children with a heart for adventure or a momentary distraction for the casual passer-by who might afford it a swift glance and a few words before moving on to more exciting things.

There is nothing particularly unusual or exceptional about this example – it's just one of the thousands dotted around the coast of England with, given the fact that the East Anglian coast was regarded by both the Allied and Axis powers as having beaches where a seaborne invasion might well take place, their proliferation along the exposed Norfolk, Suffolk and Essex coasts now, in hindsight, being both understandable and logical.

At the outbreak of the Second World War in 1939, very little thought was given to the possibility of enemy naval forces attacking or even attempting an invasion, with the only real and almost concessionary response to any perceived threat from the sea met with the installation of a 6-inch gun battery in Great Yarmouth. However, following the evacuation of the British Expeditionary Force from Dunkirk in 1940 and the subsequent fall of France, the very real proximity of a voracious enemy changed the minds of the people that mattered and the prospect of a full-blown Nazi invasion of British shores was taken very seriously indeed.

It had been deemed most likely that any attempt to do so would focus on the south coast of England, this possibility being the foundation of the popular BBC comedy *Dad's Army*, filmed on location in Norfolk but based around the town of Walmington-on-Sea, a fictional 'stand in' for Eastbourne. Yet for all this, a secondary attack on the East Anglian coast was still seen as a very real possibility, something which prompted the planning and construction of defensive fortifications across the whole of the coastline. This not only included the fortification of the region's ports (remember the SS *Vina*, taken to Great Yarmouth to be used as, if necessary, a blockship (see page 10)), but additional defensive systems built further inland.

The plan in Norfolk was relatively straightforward and involved a series of defences that included pill boxes as well as batteries, anti-tank obstacles, trenches, barbed wire, searchlights and mines, all laid in such a way so that if an invading force encountered one particular line of defensive reinforcement they would, having overcome that, then have to deal with another one. No-one expected that any form of coastal defence would halt or irrevocably thwart an aggressor's plans; instead, the intention was to delay and frustrate them for as long as possible. Defensive pill boxes, which would have been manned by a small unit of men, usually members of the local Home Guard, would play their part in that role.

Although they would have provided some protection, the pill boxes were – given the fact that they and the courageous men who manned them would be facing one of the most technologically advanced and well-trained armies in the world – not really fit for purpose, certainly as far as offering long-term and stern resistance was concerned. But they would at least provide some cover and be a place where resistance could be offered. The long-term view of the consequences of a possible invasion certainly took this into consideration as, once the coastal defences had inevitably been breached, the invading army would then be further resisted by successive 'stop lines' that were put into place further inland with the ultimate goal being to offer a very serious resistance and protection of strategic points: i.e. airfields, factories and, ultimately, major centres of population such as Norwich, which was virtually surrounded by anti-tank obstacles as well as a series of yet more pill boxes. It has since been reckoned that, countrywide, around 18,000 of them were built.

Heacham and all of the villages along the coast whose marshes and beaches contained pill boxes were ultimately seen as being expendable. Nevertheless, they would have had a role to play and there is little doubt that the people who were there to play that part would have done so with the sort of selfless courage that typified the men and women of this country at that time.

(John/APW at Shutterstock.com)

Chapter 21

Hemsby

Abandoned Holiday Camp

The popular TV series *Hi-de-Hi!* recreated rather too well the spartan surrounds and forced jollity that visitors to one of the country's holiday 'camps' (or 'parks' as they preferred to be called) would bring them for a week or two once they'd checked in. Yet, for all that, they were hugely popular, so much so that in April 1936 the Butlin's Holiday Camp in Skegness was forced to take out a newspaper advertisement announcing that, after taking 1,400 bookings in one week alone, the site had no accommodation of any kind available until mid-September.

The phenomenal early success of Butlin's was in no small part down to the introduction of the Holidays with Pay Act, which meant that all working families were entitled to a paid week off every summer. For many of them, spending that week at Butlin's, a place where everything would be provided for them, was the obvious choice and a very affordable one indeed. In 1936 a reasonable weekly wage for a manual worker was £2, which meant a week at Butlin's at around 45 shillings (£2.25) represented extraordinarily good value, especially as that cost included accommodation, food and entertainment. The holiday camp magnates couldn't lose.

One of the major rivals to the Butlin's empire was Pontins, founded and launched by Fred Pontin in 1946. His ethos was similar to that of Billy Butlin – affordable holidays for working families on a custom-built site that included everything they might possibly need for the duration. In theory, once a family booked in to the site on a Saturday morning, they had no reason to leave it until their departure date a week later. There were subtle differences. For example, the on-site entertainment staff employed to look after the families during their stay were referred to as Redcoats at Butlin's sites while at Pontins they were known as Bluecoats. Different names, identical duties and big smiles all round, even when you were cleaning up the copious piles of vomit that only an over-excited six-year-old can produce for the third time that day.

Pontins opened two adjacent sites on the Norfolk coast at Hemsby, one of which was referred to as Seacroft, while the other, larger site was simply referred to as Pontins Hemsby. At peak times, the site would house around 2,400 paying guests, all of whom had free access to the numerous attractions on offer, which included a swimming pool, boating lake, playground, amusement arcades, go-kart track, restaurant and an entertainment centre (which all children had to depart by 8 p.m.) that included a bar, stage and dance floor. Great Yarmouth might only have been 8 miles or so down the road, but why waste time and money there when everything you could possibly need for a good time was on site and within walking distance of your accommodation?

The bubble had to burst eventually. Holidays abroad became cheaper and easy to book with the added attraction of guaranteed good sunshine to accompany your day sat by the pool, something that Hemsby could never hope to promise. Visitor numbers fell year by year until, at the end of

2009, the staff working at Pontins in Hemsby were given just 48 hours' notice to leave the camp as, with little to no prior warning, it was permanently closed.

The abandoned site soon became an overgrown and derelict eyesore; a popular attraction for vandals and arsonists rather than cheerful holidaymakers in search of a good time. Its future remains, at the time of writing, unclear. Plans for it to become a residential area fell through, as did an ambitious one that would have seen it turned into the 'Eden Project of the East'. More recent plans have included one for 200 new homes as well as a space for commercial or community use.

At a site where the ethos of a community was a very important one, it would seem rather appropriate for something similar to rise from its boisterous past.

(Hugh Venables at Geograph.org.uk)

Chapter 22

Holkham

The Monument

Holkham Hall and the park that the great house stands in demand exploration. After all, who could possibly resist the temptation to enter a place that was once considered so important that all 3,000 acres of it were surrounded by a brick wall of some 9 miles in length, a foreboding edifice that was built, at the expense of many aching backs and dodgy knees, by a veritable army of hardy labourers from 1833 through to 1839.

It was initially built, of course, to keep the likes of them (as well as people like you and me) most firmly and definitely out of all the wonders that lay within. And no wonder, for the treasures that lurked within the wall included the grandiose Holkham Hall itself, as fine an example of the Palladian style (a European style of architecture derived from and inspired by Andrea Palladio, a sixteenth-century Venetian) as you will find anywhere. And eye catching it most certainly is. But you just wait until you go inside. 'Oh mio Dio', as Palladio himself might well have said.

But what is the point of having a wonderful house and equally spectacular grounds to go with it if you can't scatter the latter with a few eye-catching fripperies to accompany them? The grounds of Holkham Hall have many, of which I have selected just two (see 24) to muse upon here.

One of these is the park's monument, one which, at first glance, doesn't seem all that visually removed from its more famous half-cousin in London, which was erected 202 feet from where the Great Fire of London is said to have begun and which, in a pleasing nod towards symmetry, stands at 202 feet high.

Similar? Well, yes and no. London's monument is a Doric column whereas the one here at Holkham is a Corinthian column, another of the three principal classical orders of ancient Greek and Roman architecture, of which all things Doric are also founder members.

I've visited both. But, despite the location of London's as well as its scale and historical significance, if we are going to talk columns, Corinthian, Doric or otherwise, then I'd plump for Holkham's every time. It just looks so incongruous, soaring as it does into the (usually) clear blue skies of what is, to all extents and purposes, a back garden in rural Norfolk. A rather large back garden, I'll give you that, but a garden all the same. Somewhere you might expect to see a nice tract of lawn, a rose garden or two, a herb garden and even, at a push, an orangery. But a 124-foot-high Corinthian column? That takes a lot of *je ne sais quoi*. And then some. But there is, as you would expect at such a place, a very good reason indeed that it is there.

It was designed by the early nineteenth-century English architect William Donthorne and paid for by public subscription. The column is topped with a wheat sheaf while the square plinth at its base is decorated with panels and carvings that depict various aspects of Coke's contribution to agriculture, including seed drilling, an irrigation scheme and a Holkham sheep-shearing event in progress – an annual event at the estate that, popularity-wise, was on a par with today's Glastonbury Festival.

Coke was the proverbial big noise in agriculture at the time, a mover and shaker whose ideas and techniques in the industry reached far beyond Holkham, Norfolk and even Great Britain as a whole. The only surprise, therefore, about his monument at Holkham is not, as might be first assumed, that it is there in the first place but that it doesn't have at least the same fame and prominence as that which was erected in memory of London's Great Fire.

A worthy tribute. But you can't help thinking he deserves more.

(Ray Blyth)

Chapter 23

Holkham

The Obelisk

Norfolk has many great houses for the casual traveller to explore: Blickling, Oxburgh, Houghton and, of course, the perceived pièce de résistance at Sandringham. Yet Sandringham is anything but great in both scale and grandeur; indeed, if it wasn't for the patronage of the Royal Family, I doubt it would attract very many visitors at all. The delight of Sandringham is that you can see and feel that it is a house that is most definitely lived in with rooms that feel as if they have been suddenly vacated just before you enter them. There are indentations on the cushions and a half-finished novel or two on a convenient Louis XVI sidetable while, if you put your hand on the back of one of the TV sets that nestle among the fine art, it would probably still be warm.

Holkham is different; Holkham feels regal and glorious and, in many ways, has that monarchical feel about it that Sandringham seems to lack.

The same applies to the gardens and grounds. Sandringham's are awash with rhododendron bushes and neatly finished borders with straight edges and closely cropped grass. Even the famous statue of the Buddhist divinity Kuvera looks as if it might have come direct from a high-end garden centre. It's all very humble, simple and understated. Which is, lest you think this is a criticism (and it most certainly is not), exactly what the royals wanted it to be. King George V said of it: 'Dear old Sandringham, the place I love better than anywhere in the world.' And you can see why. It is reassuringly cosy.

The old king would probably have felt most uncomfortable among the opulence of Holkham. It was, after all, an estate which saw fit to raise a Corinthian column in memory of and to the glory of a man who revolutionised agriculture. They do pomp very well at Holkham.

Take, for example, the fine obelisk that stands due south of Holkham Hall itself. It was the first piece of work to be erected on the estate by Thomas Coke, reportedly as a symbol of intent to build a great hall on that great tract of land that he owned. Coke commissioned William Kent, the architect who had initially introduced the Palladian style of architecture into England. He was also the man behind the 'natural' style of gardening that focused more upon appreciating and working with the landscape that was there in the first place, rather than going into battle (how reassuringly British) and irrevocably changing it. Hence the rolling natural grasslands of Holkham and the precise and pristine borders, lawns and footpaths at Sandringham.

Coke didn't slavishly follow Kent's initial drawings. Maybe they were too precise and geometrical for him; perhaps he wanted something with more natural lines and even the hint of an imperfection here and there? Work started on it in 1729 and was completed three years later with the structure built amidst the gentle fields of the original village of Holkham and aligned, precisely, with the centre of Holkham Hall. This was quite a remarkable achievement when you consider that construction of the hall did not commence until two years after the obelisk had been completed and the central block of the hall, that part of the building which the obelisk is in line with, was not built until the 1740s.

The finished obelisk, which is a Grade II listed building, is 80 feet high and composed of limestone. It is another remarkable legacy of a truly remarkable man.

(Ray Blyth)

Chapter 24

Holme-next-the-Sea

Seahenge

The discovery of Seahenge on the wide-open and peaceful space that is the beach at Holme-next-the-Sea caused a lot of excitement that was, swiftly, tinged with no little controversy. Might it had been better if it had never been found at all? There are those who will certainly feel that way.

Seahenge was a 4,000-year-old timber circle dating from the Bronze Age. It had lain forgotten in sand until 1998, when the ever-present coastal forces of erosion and change were exacerbated by a combination of strong winds and high tides. Its discovery and the swift conclusion as to its age and purpose caused a huge amount of controversy when English Heritage, working alongside the admirable Norfolk Archaeological Unit, agreed to fund Seahenge's removal from the beach, choosing to do this rather than, as has since been done at the site of the Roman Fort in nearby Brancaster, opting to measure and examine it *in situ* before letting the combination of time, sea and sand cover it up again.

Many people, especially those living locally, thought that this is exactly what should have been done. Yes, of course, make use of the unique opportunity to examine and research this ancient and unique site, but once you're finished then leave it alone. You wouldn't, after all, haul Stonehenge off to a museum; why then should Seahenge be any different? It was there for a purpose and should, in the opinion of many, have been left well alone.

One concern was that Seahenge would end up in London, miles away from its 'home', and, in all likelihood, shuffled off into hidden storage somewhere once the initial interest in it had ebbed. If it was, the argument went, to be fated to a future in a cold, dark and airless place, then let it be in the sands at Holme rather than a cellar in London.

The counter argument offered was that now Seahenge was exposed, damage might accrue at the site due to its exposure to the air as well as elements of the general populace who might feel like hacking a piece of it off and taking it home with them. There is a precedent. Victorian visitors to Stonehenge were invited to do exactly that with hammer and chisels being freely provided to curious day trippers. Some objected to it being moved on religious grounds, while others felt it was just another case of the establishment turning up in Norfolk in their flash cars and fancy suits and deciding (not for the first time) that they, rather than the local people, knew best.

One high-profile objection to the site being left undisturbed was raised by the Norfolk Wildlife Trust, who pointed out that, as the timber circle lay on the edge of the Holme Dunes Nature Reserve, the crowds of people who would visit Seahenge would disturb the reserve's feeding waders and other wildlife. This was a valid point as it was estimated that around 5,000 people visited the beach in the days after the discovery – numbers that are more associated with Great Yarmouth's Pleasure Beach rather than a quiet and idyllic spot like Holme.

Cold logic eventually won the argument. Archaeologists moved on to the site and, despite a fractious relationship with objectors, began to remove the timbers within the window that tide movements allowed (usually up to 4 hours a day). They had, without their protective covering of peat and sand, already started to decay *in situ*, so were taken to the Bronze Age Centre at Flat Fen in Peterborough, where they were placed in fresh water tanks and scrupulously cleaned before being moved to the site of the Mary Rose Trust in Portsmouth where, alongside the timbers from Henry VIII's great warship, they were vacuum freeze-dried in readiness for display.

Seahenge now has a permanent home at the splendid museum in King's Lynn, which at least means it remains in its county of origin and is easily accessible to those whose distant ancestors built it in the first place

(Ken Hayes)

Chapter 25

Houghton

Water Tower

Yes, it really is 'just' a water tower. Fabulous, isn't it? A folly if ever there was one. Yet, for all the jaw-dropping wonder of this particular structure's facade, the mechanics within were an essential part of any country estate. Without a water tower on site they would have fallen into rack and ruin as that would have meant no water supply; not for the kitchens, the stables, the gardens or the good lord and lady's monthly bath. Things would have been desperate.

Mankind has, of course, always needed water. It isn't, despite what some providers of expensive and largely tasteless bottled water would like you to think, a fad or a 'must-have' accessory. It is and always will be absolutely vital to life. Not being able to access water can only mean one thing: a drawn out and rather unpleasant death. This has, throughout history, been something that has been documented again and again and again. The truth of it is that where water resources, infrastructure or sanitation systems have been unavailable or insufficient, diseases spread and people become ill and die prematurely. Major human settlements could only initially develop where there was a plentiful supply of fresh water or natural springs. Look at Europe's great cities, each and every one of them built on a river: London and the Thames; Paris and the Seine; Rome and the Tiber; Budapest and the Danube; Dublin and the Liffey. It's a long and exhausting list. No-one saw a river and thought, '...ah, we'll build here, it's a great view'. They built there because the water brought a settlement to life. It goes without saying, therefore, that man has throughout history needed to display increasingly clever and resourceful means by which communities, big and small, could always have access to their water supplies, with the greatest leap forward in relatively modern times coming via the beginnings of what we might now consider modern plumbing for the masses arriving in Britain during the Industrial Revolution. So, no more trips to the well, the pump or, if you really were out in the back of beyond, the nearest stream or river. Because the time was coming when, rather than you going to the water, the water came to you.

But hold on a moment. That age-old practice of queuing up at the village well to get your day's allowance of water (first one removes the dead cat) was all well and good if you were the working man, woman or child. Deprivation and squalor were your lot and if that meant walking a mile every morning just to get a bucketful of water, then that is what you did. If you were the Lord of the Manor, however, well that was a different matter. You couldn't possibly be expected to queue for your water with the great unwashed. No, that would have been unheard of and rather unseemly as well. The water had to come to you on demand. Like everyone and everything else did. Hence the proclivity of the very wealthy to build their own water supply systems, the evidence of which still survives on some of our great estates, with the spectacular example in the grounds of Houghton Hall being the best example of all. This water tower, or 'water house' as it would have been referred to, was, like the house itself, Palladian in design. It was built in the

1720s and stood at 41 feet high, covering, originally, a 12,000-gallon tank of lead-lined wood that was suspended just 7 feet above ground level and supplied from a well directly underneath the adjacent pump house. That original tank remained in use until the Second World War by an even larger tank, which was kept in use (and was lovingly restored under the watchful eye of the current Lord Cholmondeley's grandmother in the 1980s) until 2003, although its main purpose by then was to serve as a backup supply for the estate's firefighting service. In all, it was in use for nearly 300 years – a fitting tribute to the designers and builders of the original building.

It's also likely to be the only water tower in the world that has an open Tuscan Doric portico with stuccoed pilasters. You can try impressing your fellow visitors with that little snippet of architectural colour if you like, but no, I've no idea what it means either.

Rome has its Coliseum, Paris the Eiffel Tower and Florence the Basilica di San Lorenzo. But Houghton? Well, Houghton has its water house. And it is exquisite.

(Ray Blyth)

Chapter 26

Hunstanton

Lookout Tower

Hunstanton has the rare privilege of being a resort on the east coast of England that has a westward facing beach. It isn't, despite what some of the more spurious guidebooks would have you believe, the 'only' east coast resort in the country that can lay claim to this fact; far from it, as it isn't in reality even the only location in Norfolk that can boast glorious sunsets as part of its overall package as those devotees of the beaches at, for example, Heacham and Snettisham would strongly attest.

The devil is in the detail and all that. In any case, it is quite probable that the birdwatchers and ramblers that enjoy the peace and quiet of those villages' beaches are more than happy for Hunstanton to claim such a novel exclusive. Because that can only mean the region's hordes of pillaging pleasure seekers and holidaymakers will invariably amass there for their evening cod and chips with accompanying sunset, meaning that the flocks of birds and attendant twitchers at Snettisham continue to have 'their' beach all to themselves. A win-win situation. Particularly if you are a pink-footed goose.

Regardless of all that, it cannot be denied that if you want to see a stunning sunset then observing it from the beach at Hunstanton is about as good as it gets. And that's no hyperbole. Hollywood could spend billions of dollars trying to recreate it all as some kind of 'special effect' but they would never and could never come close to recreating the natural wonder of a Hunstanton sunset in June. It looks great from the beach or cliff tops, but what if you could have your own little private viewing space to watch it from? And not only that, one which is elevated above just about everything and everyone else in the town.

Ladies and gentlemen, I give you the coastal lookout tower at Hunstanton.

It was built in 1906 as a Marconi Wireless Station, one of a large number constructed throughout the country during the early years of the twentieth century in order to help tap in to the commercial possibilities of radio. The position at Hunstanton was, of course, a favourable one as it was sat atop a high cliff top with uninterrupted views over the Wash. A glorious site picked for its practical possibilities rather than the view.

The listening station came into its own during the First World War when it was used to gather military intelligence by intercepting German radio transmissions and, in doing so, helping trace the location of the German fleet. This was a critical responsibility when one considers that the British Royal Navy, previously thought of as being peerless in its dominion over the world's oceans, was now expected to go into battle against a German Imperial Navy that consisted of twenty-two pre-dreadnoughts (sea-going battleships built between the mid- to late 1880s and 1905), fourteen dreadnought battleships and four battlecruisers – a formidable array of naval hardware that the Royal Navy could not even think about engaging without having some intelligence about its strength and whereabouts. This meant listening posts such as this one at Hunstanton became as vital a part of the war effort as the ships themselves. This role was repeated during the Second World War (no doubt the station would have been in close contact with the personnel based at RAF Barrow Common, see page 20) when it was used as a signal station – one that received the royal 'seal of approval' in 1943 when it was visited by King George VI and Queen Elizabeth, together with Princesses Elizabeth and Margaret, who spent some time with the Coastguard before adding their names into the Coastguard's log book.

The lookout tower was became a maritime museum in 1976 before it was purchased by new owners, who undertook a thorough and very considerate restoration of the entire building, ensuring in the process that its original features remained in place. It can now be rented out by holidaymakers with a yearning for a sea view and comes complete with its own Second World War pillbox (see 21) on site.

(Ray Blyth)

Chapter 27

Hunstanton

St Edmund's Chapel

Few visitors to Hunstanton can resist the urge to take a photograph of Hunstanton's fine nineteenth-century lighthouse using the surviving arch of what is left of St Edmund's Chapel to frame it as it stands, resolute and stern against all too frequently angry skies. And why not? It's all too rare to capture two famous landmarks in one shot, the old and the (relatively) new; two coastal havens, one with the intent of bringing the faithful to God, the other with a slightly different brief of keeping them out of his reach for a little bit longer if at all possible.

St Edmund, aka Edmund of East Anglia or Edmund the Martyr, is said to have been the King of East Anglia from about 855 (and that's AD not AM – this was a very long time ago, so details are a little patchy) until his death in 869. Norfolk can lay claim to him as one of its own (Boudicca, Edmund and Lord Nelson, not a bad trio to have by your side if needed), the son of a slightly more obscure local king by the name of Æthelweard, who Edmund succeeded when he was just fourteen years old.

Contemporary accounts indicate that he was the proverbial wise and gentle monarch who cared greatly for his people and was suitably God-fearing – a belief that flew in the face of the invading Vikings at this time who, enraged at both Edmund's tendency to lead his armies into battle against them as well as his steadfast refusal to renounce Christ, beheaded him on the orders of (and this is where the whole thing starts to sound like an episode of *Game of Thrones*) one Ivar the Boneless, a notorious Viking bully who wasn't up to anything very much unless he could call upon the company and support of Ubba, his equally unpleasant brother.

I can't help but admire Edmund. He stood up for what he believed in, led from the front and was, by all accounts, a popular and respected king. And let's face it, British history is littered with quite a few dreadful ones who were everything that Edmund was not. Recognition of his courage and devotion to God led eventually (Norfolk people won't be hurried into anything) to the chapel atop the cliffs at Hunstanton to be built and dedicated to him in 1272 with the impressive arch-cum-frame still standing today along with the remains of some of the chapel's walls. A far worthier candidate to be the patron Saint of England than the current one perhaps? I think so. St Edmund's day, anyone?

Major excavations were carried out on the site in 1913. This saw many ancient artefacts recovered, including fragments of fifteenth-century window glass as well as glazed floor tiles from the fifteenth and sixteenth centuries, these discoveries indicating that the chapel was a busy and well-maintained building for at least two centuries after its initial construction and, in all probability, for some considerable time after that.

Hunstanton is rightly proud of its connection with St Edmund. As well as the chapel, the town has two streets and two churches that are named after him, while some people live in hope that, one day, the town will revert back to its original and rather beautiful name of Hunstanton St Edmund's. I'd be the first to concur with that.

(Ray Blyth)

Chapter 28

Hunstanton

The Cross

It's a fairly safe bet to assume that this particular local landmark has had more feet running up and down it, and more weary backsides taking the opportunity to sit on it in order just to take in the view it affords, than just about any other location mentioned in this book.

It is certainly user-friendly and accessible with just a hint of permanence about it. It hasn't, of course, always been sat atop Hunstanton Green, it just feels as if it has. Yet, modest as it is in size and aspect, if it were to somehow vanish overnight then Hunstanton would never quite feel the same place again.

Its current position on the town green owes much to the influence of one Henry L'Estrange Styleman Le Strange, a decorative painter by trade who was, despite his flamboyant name, a local man who was born in the town in 1815 as plain Henry Styleman. His place of birth was what is now known as Old Hunstanton, a quiet and exceedingly pretty village today that, nonetheless, is a settlement where the sight, sound and influence of the nearby sea was negligible.

Clearly born with a flair for entrepreneurship, Styleman could not stop thinking about the commercial possibilities a settlement much nearer to The Wash would bring. With this in mind – and quite possibly, given the massive physical and economic growth in and around other British resorts at this time, worried that someone else might beat him to it – he swiftly got to work on persuading a number of likeminded men to fund the construction of a railway line from King's Lynn to the town – one that would, he was convinced, be popular with tourists.

His instincts were soon proved to be spot on as the newly formed Lynn & Hunstanton Railway swiftly became one of the most successful and profitable railway companies in the country, with visitors flocking in from the Midlands in particular to take advantage of the new resort's beach, invigorating air and even more invigorating waters.

The newly renamed Le Strange didn't quite plant a victor's flag in the middle of the new and growing town to symbolise his dominion over what was now known as New Hunstanton, but he did make his mark in another way. In 1846, he moved the ancient village cross which had, for time immemorial, stood in Old Hunstanton on a site known as Gipsies Green to its present site. Lesser men may have felt that they might be subject to some kind of curse by moving such an ancient object from a place with that name, but Le Strange had no such fears and, to further mark his intentions for the new town, commissioned the building of a hotel, initially known as the Royal Hotel but known today as the Golden Lion. Situated atop that sloping green that led down to the sea, the hotel was, incidentally, referred to as 'Le Strange's Folly' for many years afterwards.

The cross was later set atop the modern steps on which it stands today. It's an easy climb to the pinnacle, from which you can look either straight ahead to the grey and occasionally treacherous waters of The Wash (where a king lost his treasure) or, just behind you, Le Strange's so called 'folly' and the handsome facade of the Golden Lion hotel.

Le Strange's name has been immortalised at another Hunstanton hotel, the Le Strange Arms. Situated on the outskirts of the town, and with commanding views over The Wash, it is as good a place as any to sit and enjoy a quiet evening drink as you join the thousands of other visitors to the town who come to indulge in one of Hunstanton's famous sunsets – a scenario that the young Henry Styleman worked out for himself at a very early age.

(Ray Blyth)

Chapter 29

King's Lynn

Greyfriars Tower

King's Lynn is a hugely underrated and, in some ways, unappreciated town. For many a visitor to Norfolk, it is little more than a point on a map or, heaven forbid, a cue for the dreaded Satnav – a point of reference as you dash past it en route to those fashionable towns and villages along the A149* and beyond. It's is a shame, because it is a town that has a lot to offer the curious explorer.

Take, for example, Greyfriars, built in 1235 and the remains of what was once an undoubtedly splendid Franciscan friary in the town. The Franciscan order, known as the Greyfriars from the colour of the robes that they wore, really were advocates of practicing what they preached, establishing this and other abbeys as close to the centre of major town populations as they possibly could so that they could live, work, preach and teach in among the good people of Bishop's Lynn (as the town was known until 1537) on a day-to-day basis.

This was in direct contrast to other monastic orders like the Cistercians for example, who preferred to establish their abbeys in far more remote areas – sometimes, no doubt, in the hope that nothing so wretched as the common man would ever come along to disturb their quiet life of prayer, brewing and generally just hanging out together. The Greyfriars were much more accommodating as an order and even went as far as to take vows of poverty and rely on donations from local people in order to survive, rather than live in opulence. They sound very pleasant and affable fellows. Friar Tuck would have fitted in well there.

By 1325, the friary supported thirty-eight friars – evidence in itself that their humble way of living and reliance on charity was working. But, humble or not, they were also resourceful and had by that time designed and built a system of conduits that brought them a supply of fresh water from a spring over a mile away. However, as pleasant and affable as they might have been, this didn't save them or their abbey from being subjected to the worst excesses of Henry VIII's hooligans on horseback during the Reformation in 1538, a fate that was also suffered by the town's three other friaries.

Yet the most significant part of the Greyfriars complex, the fifteenth-century bell tower of the friary church, was spared destruction as it was considered to be an important local landmark for sailors entering the port at the town as it was clearly visible as part of Lynn's skyline – as, indeed, it is to this day.

It is one of only three surviving Franciscan monastery towers in England, and of those three (the others are in Coventry and Richmond in North Yorkshire) it is considered to be the finest example. It stands at 93 feet high and has, in recent years, found itself dubbed with the unfortunate sobriquet 'The Leaning Tower of Lynn' as it had, over time, started to tilt at an angle of around one and a half degrees to the north-east – hardly surprising really, as the site it had been built on was marshy ground in the first place.

This potential problem was negated in 2003 when the tower was one of the finalists in the BBC TV programme *Restoration*. The publicity that this garnered eventually led to a Heritage Lottery Fund being granted to the tower, which meant vital work could be carried out on both it and the gardens it stands in. Even more importantly than that, the money also allowed for the tower's foundations and walls to be stabilised so that its tendency to lean would be stopped in its tracks (for reference, the Leaning Tower of Pisa leans at an angle of around 3.99 degrees, although it has been as much as 5.5 degrees).

A happy ending then at a site that is just one of the numerous hidden treasures which King's Lynn has to offer.

*I heartily recommend the book *A149 Landmarks* (Amberley Publishing) if you'd like to learn more about this famous old road.

(Ray Blyth)

Chapter 30

King's Lynn

Red Mount Chapel

If you aren't that familiar with King's Lynn (and if that is the case, please endeavour to put that right as soon as possible) then you won't know that there is a rather lovely area of green space in the centre of the town that is known as The Walks.

The Walks is the only surviving eighteenth-century town walk left in Norfolk. The park covers an area of 42 acres and was designated as a Grade II historic park by English Heritage in 1998. The Red Mount is the highest point in The Walks and affords a panoramic view of the entire area from the top; a welcome oasis of walks, trees and picnic spots can be seen, which helps to add a pastoral tinge to this historic old town – one that has, upon further exploration, a little bit of everything to offer the first-time visitor.

But tarry a while here and consider the Red Mount Chapel that was built on top of the mound in the late fifteenth century. It's full and rather sumptuous title is the Chapel of St Mary on the Mount, but it has long since been referred to as the Red Mount Chapel. It is a scheduled ancient monument as well as a Grade I listed building. Red Mount served as a wayside chapel for pilgrims who were journeying towards the shrine of Our Lady of Walsingham, which is around 25 miles north-east of King's Lynn. You can only imagine the excitement that those weary pilgrims must have felt upon seeing Red Mount for the first time as it would have been a significant landmark on their journey; one that not only indicated that they were now in the same English county as their ultimate goal, but that, all being well, they were – fitness and road conditions permitting – just one day's travel away from Walsingham.

Red Mount must have been a joyful place to know and be part of in those days; full of hope, happy chatter and optimism. Yet its construction and purpose were no accident. Going on a pilgrimage was a big business in the fifteenth century and, with Walsingham being the second most holy shrine in England after Canterbury, a steadily growing number of people were choosing to make the trip to Norfolk from not just all over England, but all of the Christian countries in Europe.

You cannot blame anyone for thinking that a conveniently sited stopping off place for the weary, lame and sick would be a good idea. In among all the weary, lame and sick pilgrims, there would have been a fair smattering of wealthy and influential ones, all of whom were more than prepared to pay their way into heaven if necessary. Norfolk has more than its fair share of wool churches that serve as evidence of their guilt-led largesse.

Donations would have been made by those travellers at Red Mount, and they would have been more than gratefully accepted. Its presence also brought welcome trade to the town, especially if pilgrims decided to spend one or two days in Lynn before moving on again. So yes, while it was, and remains, a holy site and one built to the glory of Mary, Mother of God, don't think that its construction was driven by faith and devotion alone. It was also a decision made with commerce and profit in mind.

Red Mount, unlike the nearby Greyfriars Priory (see 30), survived the Reformation. It therefore continued to serve the needs of man, as well as God, throughout history. In 1641, for example, it was used to store eighteen barrels of gunpowder that would ultimately be used during the English Civil War, while in 1665 it was pressed into use as a charnel house during the Great Plague. It also provided a scenic backdrop to the author and a young lady he was rather fond of at the time as they enjoyed a lunchtime picnic at some point there in the 1980s.

You can visit it yourself now during the spring and summer months and it won't cost you a penny. It is well worth a look.

(Ray Blyth)

Chapter 31

Long Melford

Kentwell Hall Dovecote

Kentwell Hall is another rather splendid stately home that has its origins as far back as the late eleventh century – a boast that sets it apart from most of its peers in both East Anglia and across England as a whole. That early reference to Kentwell can be found in the Domesday Book of 1086, which states that a manor at Kentwell formed part of a rather extensive property portfolio belonging to a man named Frodo, the brother of Abbot Baldwin of the Abbey of St Edmunds. Frodo would have been one of the most powerful and influential men in the area. It would have helped, of course, that he had a brother in a higher than usual place and there can be little doubt that the two of them maintained a 'you scratch my back, I'll scratch yours' relationship in order to healthily fulfil their respective aims, with Baldwin's lifestyle lightyears removed from that of the Greyfriars monks in King's Lynn. They led simple lives of prayer coupled with working in the community while Frodo and Baldwin would have preferred the good things in life. Most of the current facade at Kentwell dates from the mid-sixteenth century, although its colourful history really comes to life in the early part of the seventeenth century when it became, through marriage, the home of Sir Simonds D'Ewes in 1618, a lawyer who was fortunate enough to marry into the Clopton family, the owners of Kentwell at the time. D'Ewes displayed quite a tender and even sentimental side to his character following the wedding, barely able it seems to believe his good luck and fortune in marrying into such a wealthy and influential family and marking the occasion accordingly by collecting and storing as many of the family's personal papers as he could get his hands on; namely, the seventeenth-century versions of shopping lists, bills of sale, staff records and myriad other documents and letters. These provide today a rich and highly detailed record of what day-to-day life at Kentwell would have been like and have gone on to provide the hall with the foundation for the famous recreations of seventeenth-century life that are now a regular and very popular feature at Kentwell.

When you first cast your eyes upon the dovecote at Kentwell, you'd be forgiven for thinking it was a small but rather lovely outbuilding that might have been used as a lodge or perhaps some sort of bijou accommodation for guests who wanted to get away from all the affairs and accoutrements of the 'big house'. But no, it really is a dovecote, and as you step inside you'll note it is a multi-storey dovecote that contains enough space for a veritable squadron of doves in just about the most spectacular bird house that you'll see anywhere. It is completely over the top, of course, but with good reason. Doves, along with pigeons, were given such extravagant accommodation in return for their eggs, flesh and, maybe most importantly of all, their droppings, which were used as both a fertiliser and, because of their high saltpetre content, as a constituent part of gunpowder. It is little wonder, therefore, that any self-respecting manor lord valued his doves and pigeon flocks very highly; so much so that if the proverbial common man was thought to have taken one for his pot then, starving or not, the justice meted out to him would have been extremely severe. Kentwell's dovecote spared no expense; indeed, there is room inside for 144 nesting boxes on each wall, as well as a revolving access ladder.

The possession of a dovecote was also symbolic of the status and power that the owner of the estate that it stood upon wished to, quite literally, show off, with the logic being that if something as humble as a dovecote can still be this large, spectacular and expensive, then just think how rich and powerful I must be. Owning and erecting a dovecote was a special privilege that wasn't freely given, being referred to as *droit de colombier*, which translates as having the right to own one. This was done to ensure that only the privileged few could have dovecotes, which meant that, with hardly any other dovecotes in the immediate area, Kentwell's would have had a virtual monopoly on all the birds (and therefore all the benefits and profits) in the area. The internal wall on one side of the dovecote collapsed due to wind in a storm in the winter of 2017/18 but has since been rebuilt.

We may consider doves and pigeons pests today, but they were anything but that in Kentwell's heyday and, far from being an inconvenience, were regarded as extremely valuable commodities – something which the scale and opulence of this particular dovecote illustrates very well indeed.

(Ray Blyth)

Chapter 32

Long Melford

Melford Hall Octagon

We're already beginning to learn that the myriad owners of Kentwell Hall have always believed in the mantra that if you want to build something well, then build it bigger and better than anyone else's in the neighbourhood. Even the upper classes were avid followers of the concept of 'keeping up with the Joneses' – or, as it might have been at Kentwell, keeping up with the Withipolls and Gosnolds.

Pity then the owners at nearby Melford Hall in the same village. It's roots, unlike Kentwell's, do not go back as far as the Domesday Book but, nevertheless, it still dates back to the sixteenth century, incorporating in its construction parts of a medieval building that had previously been held by the abbots of Bury St Edmunds – remember our old friend Abbot Baldwin and Frodo, his Tolkienesque brother?

The abbey suffered an ignominious fate during the Reformation when, its cessation as a place of worship confirmed, Queen Mary granted the site to a Sir William Cordell, who had spent much of his early life at Kentwell, where his father was a steward. William proved to be a popular and well-liked boy as far as the Cloptons, the owners of Kentwell, were concerned – so much so that they sponsored him to go to London to train as a lawyer. Mary's generosity in then granting the estate at Melford came about after Sir William had used his position in order to help her accede to the throne.

Cordell dutifully rebuilt and modified Melford, making it over his lifetime a grand and very impressive family home – one that was even visited by Queen Elizabeth I in 1578. This regal visit would have acted as both a tribute to him and his place in society as well as the work he had carried out on the building for, much as she enjoyed her travels and making the very most of her subjects' hospitality (whether they liked it or not), the Virgin Queen was a fussy house guest and would only stay in the finest and most highfalutin' of surroundings. One likes to think a few impoverished lords might have deliberately kept their great homes in a state of some disrepair in order to avoid a visit from the queen and her voracious and ever-growing court as well as its assorted followers and hangers-on.

She wouldn't, however, have had the opportunity to enjoy the finest dining that Melford would have had to offer (with bird meat fresh from the dovecote at Kentwell, presumably?) during her stay however, as Melford Hall's Octagon dates back to the early seventeenth century. Octagon buildings and structures are of course characterised by that very shape (i.e. they are planned and built as an eight-sided building with approximately equal sides), with one of the earliest known octagon buildings being the Tower of Winds in Athens, which dates back to around 300 BC. With such classical overtones, it's hardly surprising that having an octagon in your grounds soon caught on among the great and the good in the same way that orangeries and Doric temples had.

There were early precedents. The Abbot's Kitchen in Oxford dates back to the fourteenth century, while Wells Cathedral has an octagonal chapter house. In addition to that, Ely Cathedral, not that distant from Melford, has its famous octagonal lantern tower.

There are plenty more such examples of octagonal buildings throughout England. Melford's is relatively modest when compared to octagons that form part of the great building that is a cathedral or castle. Nonetheless, as a standalone building it was, and remains, very impressive. Functionally, it was intimate with its contents said to have been a marble table and just five gilt wood chairs. A private dining space for the family then – a very upmarket summer house, even – but a wonderful building in its own right.

(Ray Blyth)

Chapter 33

Long Melford

Water Conduit

A water conduit is a channel or pipe used for the conveyance of water to a terminal point which, in more instances than not, is something as simple as a tap. We all, therefore, have our very own water conduits, the pipes that supply it to the various outlets and conveniences in our homes that supply water, whether that be a sink, bath, WC, garden tap or washing machine. It is simple and something we all take for granted, unless, of course, the supply is lost and we can no longer get water as and when we want it. Then all hell can break loose. Those among us with long memories will remember the great drought of 1976, when shortages of water meant queuing up at a standpipe in the street to collect whatever you needed in bottles, pails and other hastily convened containers – a situation that people were not very happy about, to say the least. Were something similar to happen today, the internet would, in all probability, melt in protest. Yet that was how people used to collect their water, each and every day, without fail. If you didn't or couldn't go, then you did without, and that could be serious.

Melford Hall obtained its water through a supply 'guarded' by this Grade II* listed sixteenth-century Tudor red brick water conduit. In its design and appearance we see, yet again, how the owners of East Anglia's great houses liked to show off. Doric temples, orangeries, a pyramid and a dovecote with bespoke, readymade roosts for hundreds of birds. And lots more besides that. Is it taking things to excess? Yes, quite possibly. At a time when a lot of people barely had a home to go to and were, for the most part, going hungry, the flagrant display of wealth and power given out by some of the owners of our great homes seems insensitive at best and downright callous at worse.

By the middle of the nineteenth century, much of continental Europe had put up with the myriad disparities between 'them and us' for long enough, with the revolutions of 1848 symptomatic of a people that wanted more than a mere hand to mouth existence. France had long done away with Marie Antoinette of course while, in 1917, the rule of the Tsars in Russia came to an abrupt and bloody end. The peasants really were revolting – and rightly so. Except, that is, for those in Britain, where respect for the system that kept the people 'in their place' more or less stayed in place. This meant that the great houses that stood as their symbolic masters remained *in situ* and can still be seen and enjoyed to this day, orangeries and all.

I don't know quite how we put up with all of those symbols of uncontrolled wealth, greed and power for quite so long. It may have helped, as far as the owners of Melford Hall were concerned, that they seemed quite willing to turn a blind eye to the fact that the villages of Long Melford would regularly and quite openly visit what had been constructed as the exclusive water source for the hall to take some for their own use. Technically they were stealing from the 'big house' and might have expected to receive hefty sanctions in return. Yet they were able to use this conduit with relative impunity. It wasn't as if there wasn't an alternative supply for them either as there was one in the village churchyard; yet most locals refused to use this, the argument being that the supply there was tainted by the dead bodies that lay there. On the other hand of course, if the alternative source of supply in the village was good enough for the 'nobs' then it must be safe enough for them to use as well. Impeccable logic.

Pleasingly, the building that houses the conduit, which was built at the same time as Melford Hall, was also designed to replicate the style used in the building of the hall itself. It is based on a square plan with octagonal corner buttresses, each of which have their own capped octagonal turrets. A mini-castle in other words and a building that, for both its humble size and purpose, is very pleasing to the eye indeed; just as it would have been for the thirsty inhabitants of Long Melford at that time who were able to sup at the same well as their supposed betters. It is refreshing in more ways than one.

(Ray Blyth)

Chapter 34

Norfolk Broads

The Norfolk Broads

I love the Norfolk Broads. Admittedly, they're not as visually dramatic as the Lake District or as wild and gloriously isolated as the Yorkshire Moors, the latter being another favourite of mine – the glory that is Roseberry Topping in particular. But if you want mood, if you want atmosphere and romance, then the Broads are hard to beat. After all, didn't David Bowie see fit to namecheck them in one of his most famous songs?*

It's hard to realise that the Norfolk Broads are, in fact, a ruin. But they are. Those calm lakes and the six interlinking rivers that conjoin them (Ant, Bure, Chet, Thurne, Waveney and Yare) that are enjoyed by so many people today are the remains of a mighty medieval industry, as much the remains of a job creator and money maker as the steelyards and coalfields of northern England once were before they too succumbed to their fate, the difference being that the one suffered here was caused by natural rather than economic causes.

As National Parks go (the Norfolk Broads are part of the family that includes Britain's other National Parks although they do not share their legal status), their origins are fairly recent. Indeed, in geological terms they came into existence before you even started to read this paragraph. They are not the product of age-old geological forces and thousands of years of history are not imbued in their dark waters; they are, in fact artificial features; flooded medieval peat excavations and a one-time shop floor that exist as a legacy of the enormous business that peat was during that time, the sometimes almost unfeasible and voracious demands for it including Norwich Cathedral, requiring nearly 320,000 tons of peat a year. Now that's an eyebrow-raising total in itself but it sounds even more remarkable when you do the maths and consider that means the good folk at the cathedral were burning their way through it at an approximate rate of around 36 tons per day, which equates to a little over five full-grown African elephants.

The good people of Norfolk started to excavate these peat pits in the twelfth century with the region's local monasteries particularly keen to secure the legal rights to do so in the areas they had influence over. The abbots had swiftly realised, no doubt, just how much of a lucrative business peat would become. And it most certainly did. But that was a downside; as the diggings became ever deeper and spread over a wider area, the water levels, inexorably, began to rise and the pits began to flood.

No-one wanted that to happen and attempts were made to quell the flooding in order for this lucrative business to remain a growing (or, rather, digging) concern. Wind pumps were hastily built and dykes were dug while the abbots and attendant monks would, have no doubts about this, prayed regularly and desperately for a solution to their watery woes. But it was all to no avail. By the fourteenth century the whole area was almost completely flooded and the industry was abandoned, with the landscape ultimately evolving into the one that we see today, with its reed beds, grazing marshes and wet woodlands.

What originated as medieval peat diggings became the largest area of protected wetland in the UK, one that covers an area of more than 110 square miles. So think about it the next time you walk or sail upon the Norfolk Broads. It is a place of leisure and enjoyment now, but once upon a time it was a thriving and hugely profitable area of industry that experienced some remarkable boom years; one that, ultimately, Mother Nature wanted to take back.

Life on Mars

(Mark Oakden at www.tournorfolk.co.uk)

Chapter 35

Norfolk Broads

St Benet's Abbey

A site and scene to make a writer weep with pleasure, such are the stories it could evoke – real or imagined, or a bit of both. Any ruin is going to look good on the Broads. They stand stark against the skyline, remote from 'civilisation' in many cases, silent and lonely sentinels of a time when the Broads buzzed to trade rather than tourists and when opportunists of all shapes, sizes and persuasions looked to make their presence felt in this part of Norfolk, located, as it was, close to Norwich, which for a while became second only to London in terms of importance and influence.

The evocative ruin here is that of St Benet's Abbey, a monastery of the Order of St Benedict. It's situated, strategically, close to the banks where the rivers Bure and Ant meet. The only Norfolk monastery founded in the Anglo-Saxon period which prospered right into the Middle Ages, it – like so many other sites at this time – began its fall into a ruinous state prior to the Reformation, which brought no reprieve for its decaying state in the way that had benefitted others: for example, at Ely where, post-Reformation, the Cathedral was 'redeployed' as the new parish church for the town. Thus, instead of being absorbed into the newly formed Church of England, the site was largely abandoned, primarily because of its remote and largely inaccessible location.

The abbey had seen a glorious past prior to its demise, being the fulcrum of one of the wealthiest Benedictine monasteries in the country – a wealth secured by its near total control of all the peat diggings (see 35), whose origins eventually led to the existence of the Norfolk Broads that we know today. But not only that; these were monks who believed in diversification in business and they additionally oversaw and profited from farming and myriad other industries in the area.

Perhaps its obvious financial profitability and success was one of the reasons that Henry VIII saw fit to look kindly upon St Benet's during the Reformation. Its slide into decline had already began by then, but instead of closing it the monarch appointed a new bishop to the site in return for some land that was owned by the Diocese of Norwich: a sensible and practical alternative to a lot of unpleasantness all round, then. Except that this turned out to be far from the case as the new bishop promptly plundered the site of all its valuables, an act which saw the last monk leave soon afterwards and the demolition of the abbey begin in earnest.

The drainage mill was originally used to crush coleseed (the seed of the rape plant, that bright yellow flower that splashes the May countryside with a sea of colour), which used to make oil for lamps before being converted into a drainage pump. It is reputed to be the oldest tower mill remaining on the Norfolk Broads today.

The present-day Bishop of Norwich retains the title of Abbot of St Benet's and continues with the tradition of holding one service a year on the site, one that began in 1939. It is truly splendid in its isolation. Don't forget to take your camera.

(BMA at Shutterstock.com)

Chapter 36

Norwich

Cow Tower

Norwich is a captivating place that has so much history and character to offer the curious explorer that it could probably afford to lend some of its lesser known delights to a city that is not quite as fortunate with regards to the items of interest it has to offer.

Cow Tower might be one of them. It'd be a focal point of interest in a lot of places, somewhere that had a small gift shop and café lurking in its shadow as coachloads of tourists made their way around it, quietly agog at both its significance and magnificence.

In reality it ekes out a tranquil existence by the River Wensum, a familiar sight to joggers who might pass it without even a first glance while unsuspecting visitors out for a quiet walk by the river might see it suddenly hove into view and wonder what on earth they have stumbled upon.

What they will be looking at is one of the earliest built artillery blockhouses (a small fort) in England, one that was built in around 1398 in order to defend Norwich from any aggressive forces, French or otherwise, who chose to use the river as a means of nefarious entry to the prosperous city centre.

As 'small' forts go, Cow Tower is quite a big one. It's height of around 50 feet was not only intended to give the fort's inhabitants a good view of what might be happening on the opposite bank of the river, but to also give anyone with mischief in mind a visual reminder of what they would be letting themselves in for if they fancied a scrap: don't mess with us.

Cow Tower was, from a military point of view, the Challenger 2 of its time. It was intended to not only house guns and a garrison, but could also be utilised by soldiers armed with small guns or even crossbow with arrow loops (narrow openings or crosses set inside walls and towers) incorporated into the build to permit this. The walls were built with a core of mortared flint rubble that was faced internally and externally with brick along with external stone dressings. When Cow Tower was garrisoned, it is likely that the ground floor served as a communal dining room, with the soldiers being provided with sleeping quarters on the upper two levels. It was, for the fourteenth century, state-of-the-art stuff.

The fort played a role in the famous Kett's Rebellion of 1549 when the rebels attacked Norwich with artillery, damaging in the process the tower's parapets. Repairs to the tower walls were eventually carried out in the late nineteenth century, but, as was sometimes the case with items of historical interest at this time (remember the Victorians taking their hammer and chisels to Stonehenge?), the work was somewhat slapdash and ended up doing more harm than good to the structure. The tower's long-term future was eventually assured in 1953 when it was taken into the guardianship of the Ministry of Works, who were able to stabilise its condition, although not to the extent of managing to restore or recover the floors and roof of the building, which have been lost. It is now jointly managed by English Heritage and Norwich City Council.

Why Cow Tower? The most likely explanation to the fort's unusual name (not one that would, after all, terrorise the heart of an enemy at its mere suggestion) is that it was derived from the surrounding meadows, which were known as Cowsholme.

(Mark Newstead)

Chapter 37

Norwich

The Nest

You want to build a football stadium; one that has a capacity for around 25,000 people – so a fairly substantial one at that. The very last place you would look to locate one would be in a disused chalk pit glorified in the name of Rump's Hole. It neither sounded nor looked appealing. Nothing, as they say, to see here. Move along please. Except, of course, they 'do diff'rent' in Norfolk. Rump's Hole? Disused chalk pit? A lack of space? Precipitous drops? Perfect, we'll take it!

And thus The Nest, the unique ground of Norwich City from 1908 to 1935, was born. It's more of a memory than even a ruin today but there is a plaque on a nearby wall to look at if you want to track it down and find the site which was home to what was, and remains, the most unusual ground in the history of British football.

Setting a football stadium within the confines of a quarry was never going to be easy and The Nest was no exception. It was cramped (an estate agent would have called it 'bijou') to say the least and little short of ramshackle, even when it had just been built. There was little to no space at the sides of the pitch while the terraces and stands that were precariously perched at its perimeter had to be squeezed into whatever space was available. Alongside one side of the pitch was a 50-foot-high concrete wall with, immediately behind that, a sheer cliff face and a terrace on top of that cliff. Who needs Health and Safety? Not the football fans of the early decades of the twentieth century, that's for certain. They laughed in its face in a rumbustious manner before taking to their rattles and peering over the edge of oblivion as the Canaries mounted another attack.

If it was a potentially dangerous experience for the fans then the players didn't always get off scot-free either. Recalling the days when he played for the Canaries at The Nest, Bernard Robinson described it as '… a shocking ground, never a professional football ground … I think it must have been very intimidating for teams that weren't used to it, especially wingers. They were probably only about 5 feet away from the crowd. Did people swear at them? Oh my word, yes'.*

When the FA eventually informed the Canary hierarchy that their ground really wasn't fit for purpose, the Club Chairman, John Pyke, argued for their staying put and spoke of redesigning The Nest with the help of Archibald Leach, the famous stadium architect behind Villa Park in Birmingham and Ibrox, home of Glasgow Rangers. Pyke's plans included, unfeasibly, almost doubling the existing ground's capacity to around 45,000, claiming that it would still be cheaper than moving to a new ground. He was, however, outvoted on the matter by his board of directors who had also considered moving into the city's greyhound stadium as an alternative before deciding that a brand-new ground was the best option. Cue the inevitable gags about the Canaries going to the dogs.

The new ground at Carrow Road was completed in just eighty-one days, leading to the people of Norwich proudly claiming that their new ground was the 'Eighth wonder of the world'. Hyperbole? Not really when you consider that, with all the modern building materials and technology available at the time, it still took the previously mentioned FA's contractors over four years to build the current Wembley Stadium.

Part of the old Nest still lives on at Carrow Road with much of it ending up being broken up and carted across the city to be used as rubble in the building of the new terraces.

It was a refreshing, if somewhat unconventional, antidote to the bland and anodyne modern stadia in the game today.

*From 12 Canary Greats (Waghorn, Rick), Jarrold Publishing, 2004.

(Dan Brigham at Norwich City FC)

Chapter 38

Near Cromer

Railway Bridge

I've stretched the definition of 'folly' for this book. I know that and I am sure that any and all folly purists keen to stress that point will not hesitate to let me know. That doesn't worry me. I've used it here to describe any building or structure that merits more than a look; one that catches the eye and plays with the imagination – whether that be for its audacity, its splendour or the logic behind it, strange as that may often seem – or, as is the case with this railway bridge, one whose very design and construction should take your breath away.

You'll be familiar with this bridge if you travel on the Bittern Line, that wonderful stretch of rural railway that runs from Norwich to Cromer and Sheringham; familiar, that is, from the point of view of someone going across it. The view is fleeting and you know that you are on a bridge of some kind, but for most people that will be it. So let's take the view of someone who isn't on the bridge and take a look up at it instead. What an astonishing feat of engineering it is: while purely functional, it is as majestic as any stately home or noble castle ruin.

The Bittern Line was opened between Norwich and North Walsham in 1874 by the East Norfolk Railway with the extension to Cromer following in 1877, meaning that this fine old bridge can be dated to around that year. It is a serviceable piece of Victorian engineering that is still being used to this day – and by trains that are bigger and heavier than their nineteenth-century counterparts, such as the hefty diesel unit crossing it in the photograph.

Modern roads that are no more than a decade old are plagued by potholes and forever subject to repair and degradation. Would that they could have been designed and built by the sort of men who had the minds and imagination to construct this bridge. It wasn't, for them, a gap that couldn't be crossed. The top hats and bean counters at the East Norfolk Railway wanted an extension through to Cromer so that was it: the extension would be built and if a bridge, however big and grand, had to be built to help achieve that purpose, then it would be built.

The line between Cromer and Sheringham, where it terminates, was opened in 1877 using a section of the Midland & Great Northern Joint Railway, one of many that criss-crossed Norfolk at the time in the same manner that wild animal tracks randomly decorate virgin snow on an icy January morning. Nearly all of them are gone now, which was, is, and will always be a tragedy. But at least this line and this bridge survives.

Like its counterparts on the outskirts of East Runton, two more mighty tributes to Victorian engineering genius, this bridge is largely hidden to the wider public view and unappreciated, which is a great pity because they are sublime. If you find yourself near one of these great beasts, take the time to walk right up to it and stand up close to the brickwork. Look up, look around you, smell the air, feel the texture of the masonry. It's like being in some great rural cathedral, one that you may well be privileged enough to have all to yourself. Except that other chap there with his camera may well be me.

(Colin Cubitt)

Chapter 39

Near Great Yarmouth

Burgh Castle

I was born and raised in Brancaster on the Norfolk coast, a village renowned for its beach and, for the sports fan, its exceptionally good golf course. Brancaster is, however, also well known for being the site of a Roman fort that was built to the east of the present village, the settlement being known at the time as *Branodunum*.

Brancaster, as we soon learnt in school, made up part of a coastal defensive line that was known as the Roman forts of the Saxon shore. These fortifications were dotted at strategic points along the exposed eastern coast of England from *Branodunum* at their most northerly point to *Portus Adurni* (Portsmouth) on the Channel coast, with the site of Burgh Castle, then known as *Gariannonum*, being one of the forts on that line.

No physical evidence of the fort remains at Brancaster, though you can see some of the masonry used for its construction in the walls of the nearby Parish Church of St Mary. Contrary to that, however, if you take the time and trouble to visit Burgh Castle you will be treated to one of the best preserved and most impressive Roman buildings to survive anywhere in Britain.

These forts were built by the Romans to protect Britain from the increasingly frequent attacks it was experiencing from well-equipped and well-organised seaborne raiders from across the North Sea as well as to provide a certain amount of visible security to their harbours and the merchant shipping that would have used them.

Such is the geographical and strategic significance of the site, near to a harbour and on the eastern bank of the River Waveney, that it remained throughout history one that encouraged settlement and, with it, local prosperity. Long after the Romans had departed these shores for the final time, it became the site of a Norman castle as well as an early Christian monastery, as contemporary research suggests. The latter has been postulated as the possible site of Cnobheresburg, a fort where the first Irish monastery in southern England was founded by Saint Fursey as part of a series of missions that were catalogued by none other than the Venerable Bede. He observed in his *Ecclesiastical History of the English People* that Cnobheresburg was '... established in the precinct of an old, stone-built Roman shore fort near the sea', which seriously suggests that the fabled Cnobheresburg was built at this very site, although this has long been disputed by historians (perpetual spoilers) with, as far back as 1983, the Norfolk Museums Service declaring that there is no evidence that there was ever a monastic settlement at Burgh Castle.

I prefer to think that there was. After all, prior to 1922 some historians and archaeologists were convinced that the tomb of Tutankhamen was not in Egypt's Valley of the Kings.

Take the time to visit this ancient and, quite possibly, holy site and decide for yourself. Our minds, hearts and souls are more instinctive that any theory can ever be.

It's an easy place to visit. It was bought in 1995 by the Norfolk Archaeological Trust, who own and manage this lovely site on behalf of English Heritage. What stories it could tell. Go and listen.

(Ray Blyth)

Chapter 40

Sandringham

Appleton Water Tower

Once again I find myself doffing an imaginary cap to the great planners and engineers of Victorian Britain, because this is as good an example of Victorian engineering and imagination as you will see anywhere in East Anglia. It is one that has, thankfully, been preserved since it was built in 1871 after the then Prince of Wales, later King George V, fell ill with typhoid after drinking contaminated water while staying at Londesborough Lodge near Scarborough in Yorkshire. A novel way of ensuring that you never receive a royal visit again, but no laughing matter. Even though typhoid was very much thought of as a disease of the tropics, it can, however, be contracted from any location where the levels of sanitation are poor, conditions and consequences that his father, King Edward VII, determined would affect no-one, least of all himself and his immediate family whenever they were staying at Sandringham.

The tower was built to ensure that the estate always had a supply of clean and fresh drinking water. It is 60 feet high and in its time was crowned with a cast-iron tank that contained 32,000 gallons of water – three times that of the water tower that had been built at nearby Houghton Hall (see 26) a little over 150 years earlier.

Appleton also had residential quarters built into the tower in order for a 'resident keeper of the royal water' to remain *in situ* at all times and to ensure that there would never be any problems with supply, especially if the nearby great house was hosting a banquet or taking on a number of overnight guests which would mean demand would be high. There was even a viewing room built at the very top of the tower for the use of the Royal Family, who would have their own private access to the top, thus ensuring they never had to suffer, heaven forbid, an encounter with the household servant who resided there.

Like Orford Castle (see 41), the tower follows a neo-Byzantine structure and used many different building stones in its construction so that it could, appearance wise, mimic some of the classic buildings from the Middle East.

All this, lest we forget, for a building that is as functional and prosaic in nature as a water tower. However, as we have already seen with the Redgate water tower in Heacham (see 20), the design and look of water towers was seemingly irresistible to Victorian and Edwardian engineers, who would make the very most of the size and bulk needed in order to make them as ornamented and ornate as possible: a clear case, it would seem, of putting your CV in the public eye and seeing what came from it.

Restoration on the tower commenced in 1976. It now serves a rather more glamorous role as one of Norfolk's more exclusive holiday rentals over four separate floors with a panoramic terrace at the top. Just don't expect the neighbours to pop round with a welcoming basket of fruit while you're there. More information about the tower can be found at www.landmarktrust.org.uk.

(Peter Barr at Geograph.org.uk)

Chapter 41

Sheringham

Repton's Temple

You may not have heard of Humphry Repton, which is a shame as that does seem to be his legacy; the man whose claim to fame and glory has been usurped somewhat by Capability Brown, a name just about everyone is at least vaguely familiar with.

Repton was born in 1752, the son of a high-ranking customs official who saw his offspring developing into a textiles tycoon, so much so that he financed his study in Rotterdam. Clothes and threads did not, however, appeal to Master Humphry, who soon gave up that pursuit to dally, briefly, with farming, sketching and music, none of which would likely have led to him making a fortune. He took on, again for just a short period, another career change when he agreed to take a position at the office of the Lord Lieutenant of Ireland, but this too failed to seize his imagination and he decamped to Norfolk, where he decided that he would rather like to give landscape gardening a go.

It sounds, admittedly, like just another story of a privileged young man jumping from one interest to another without really being committed to any of them. In this case, however, Repton's instincts had been correct as he combined an artistic eye with his sketching skills to become, as he called it (and the phrase originated with him), a 'landscape gardener', determining that he would fill in the gap in the market created by the recent death of Capability Brown and immediately setting out to do so by sending circulars to all of his wealthy and influential friends (who probably thought the whole thing was a bit of a hoot) advertising his services.

This paid off as in 1788 he was awarded a modest commission to design and layout Catton Park , a 70-acre site around 2 miles north of Norwich, with the main work undertaken involving overall landscaping and judicious planting of trees and shrubs. He also improved the aspect of Norwich Cathedral, which he did by removing some trees to the south of the park to provide a fine view of its spire.

His masterpiece has to be Sheringham Park, for which he presented the plans in 1812 knowing, quite possibly, that this project would be among his last and that, if that was to be the case, it could be a fitting epitaph to his work. It's fair to say that he succeeded. The park today is one of Norfolk's hidden gems, rich with mature woodlands that include maples, acers, styrax, eucryphia and a snowdrop tree as well as large and varied collection of rhododendrons and azaleas.

Repton also designed the temple that stands in the park, taking in some commanding views over the surrounding area as well as the nearby Sheringham Hall and the Norfolk coast beyond that. Unfortunately, he did not live to see this constructed, and not only that but when it was built and eventually opened in 1975, nearly 160 years after his death, it was not on the site which he had originally designated – two facts that seem to sum up the oversight that history seems to have given the man who will always be doomed to lurk in the shadows of Capability Brown. This is despite the fact that he designed the grounds for many of the foremost country homes in Great Britain, among them Blaise Castle, Gunton Hall, the Royal Pavilion in Brighton and Woburn Abbey – an impressive CV by any standards on its own.

He also has the honour of being namedropped by none other than Jane Austen, who mentions Repton by name in chapter six of *Mansfield Park* – something which most definitely would have appealed to his unquestionably artistic temperament.

(Ray Blyth)

Chapter 42

Thornham

Coal Barn

Smugglers. That's what I think of whenever I see Thornham Coal Barn. Small groups of people making their way over the creeks and sand dunes in the dead of night in order to procure whatever illicit booty might be coming their way, with plans to hide, store and sell it. Wages were meagre and the price of a decent bottle of brandy or some fine material would be a generous supplement to the income of a desperate man with a family to feed.

Thornham Coal Barn is, of course, neither a ruin nor a folly, but it is a symbol of a trade that has fallen into ruin, the trade that used to be the lifeblood of Thornham's busy and prosperous harbour, one of many that are dotted along this part of the coast, including Castle Rising, Heacham, Thornham, Brancaster Staithe, Burnham Overy Staithe, Morston and Blakeney to name just a handful of examples.

Thornham, like its peers, used to be a hive of activity. The harbour would have been a busy place from dawn to dusk as people went about their business loading or unloading goods: wheat, barley, coal, fish and a myriad other goods, all were either brought ashore and carried inland or transported from the fertile land that surrounded these villages and shipped off to customers both near and far.

A village's economy depended on the prosperity and jobs that its harbour would bring.

Now, sadly, the trade has all but disappeared. Castle Rising's harbour silted up, a fate that generated the well-known local rhyme that documented it:

> Rising was a sea-port
> When Lynn was but a marsh,
> Now Lynn it is a sea-port
> And Rising fares the worse.

Thornham's harbour hasn't suffered such an ignominious fate. The Coal Barn, an eighteenth, possibly nineteenth-century building that sits on the quayside, had a purpose as deeply utilitarian as its appearance. It was a building constructed for the purpose of storing the coal and other goods that were brought ashore at Thornham Harbour prior to their making their way to a final destination via, no doubt, the well-worn and atmospheric 'coast road' – aka the A149. And yes, maybe the occasional sack or bottle of contraband would be stowed in a secret place within or around the Coal Barn's stout walls. Better for the working man to prosper than the man from Customs & Excise.

Thornham Harbour is still busy today of course, but the din and brouhaha of a working port has been, for the most, replaced by braying boaties and their barking dogs. Better that, of course, than the silted obscurity that befell Castle Rising's harbour. And some do still prosper; the shellfish industry, for example, is a shining example of local enterprise up at Brancaster Staithe.

Tides come and go and life goes on, but that isn't always a good thing.

(Richard Humphrey at Geograph.org.uk)

Chapter 43

Walsingham

Priory Arch

Another arch, but what a noble example of its art. It still stands, defiant and proud, as a wonderfully suggestive tease as to just what might have been when Walsingham Priory was in its pomp before its destruction during the Reformation in 1538. Yes, the Reformation again. So many great and noble ruins stand as a legacy towards those acts of vandalism and violence instigated by Henry VIII and his cohorts. What even finer buildings might we have to explore today had it never happened?

The priory at Walsingham owes its origins to the time of Edward the Confessor, one of the last Anglo-Saxon kings of England who ruled from 1042 to 1066. The Shrine of Our Lady at Walsingham was established in 1061 when Richeldis de Faverches prayed to ask that she might be able to undertake some special work in honour of Our Lady. The Virgin Mary is said to have answered her prayer by leading her in spirit to Nazareth and showing her the house where the Annunciation (the moment when the Angel Gabriel informed Mary she was with child) occurred before asking her if she could build a replica in Walsingham to serve as a reminder of that moment.

The Holy House was duly built, with the Augustinian Canons seeing to the building of the priory in around 1150, the ruined arch that you can see today the lasting tribute to what was one of the great 'must-see' shrines in all of medieval Christendom. It was a place of pilgrimage that attracted followers from far and wide who would not hesitate in making what would have been an extremely arduous journey to pay their respects (Norfolk is hard enough to get to these days, imagine what it must have been like nearly 900 years ago). Unsurprisingly, the act of pilgrimage became big business that saw many entrepreneurial types set up resting places for them along the way where, for a price, they could eat and take shelter for a night or two, with the Red Mount Chapel in King's Lynn being one of them (see 31).

The shrine and priory attracted more than its fair share of monarchs all, no doubt, looking to show their subjects how pious they were while secretly hoping their devotion to the cause would grant them a place in Heaven. Henry III travelled there, as did Edward I. Likewise Edward II, Henry VII and even, in 1513, the scourge of the Catholic Church in England, King Henry VIII himself.

Such a mighty and popular place would never survive the ravages of the Reformation.

In 1538, the abbey's last abbot, Prior Vowell, saw which way the religious wind was blowing and took sides with Henry VIII, assisting the king's commissioners by agreeing that Walsingham Priory should be destroyed and arranging for the removal of the figure of Our Lady as well as many of the valuables that lay within. He was well rewarded for his treachery, receiving a pension of £100 a year for his troubles (more than a considerable fortune then).

The site was sold by the king for the sum of £90 and a private mansion was built on the land where it stood. Fortunately, the great east-end arch of the priory survived the destruction, a sad and desolate remnant of a building that must have once been among the most spectacular of its type in all of Europe.

Visiting the site in the spring and walking amidst its carpet of snowdrops is particularly recommended.

(Ray Blyth)

Chapter 44

Walsingham

Gate House

We've already established that medieval Walsingham was a rather special place. It still is today, of course. The village of Little Walsingham (I'm referring to the site here as the generic 'Walsingham' as both Little and Great are worth a visit and some of your time) creaks under the strain of thousands of pilgrims, worshippers and travellers every year – visitor numbers that you'd expect a large city or well laid-out and contemporary site to accommodate easily. Yet Walsingham still retains its charm and unique atmosphere, and even on the busiest days you can usually find an isolated spot for some quiet reflection on your own.

In medieval times, however, a trip to Walsingham was almost akin to making one to Disneyland today. It was one of the most important pilgrimage sites in the world – a rival, in the pilgrim stakes, to even mighty Rome itself. If a village could be a superstar on the world stage then Walsingham was a headline act. It is hard to believe now, perhaps, as you stroll its quiet streets, but true, nonetheless. Naturally enough, if you were a big and important place then you had to take the opportunity to show that was the case at every given opportunity.

So take, for example, the gatehouse and porter's lodge that sit on the village's High Street today. It is imposing and impressive in outlook with its own mighty arch intended, of course, to help support the great weight of the upper part of the building atop it, all flint rubble with local dressings. Within that arch is another, a four-centered archway (also known as a depressed arch, a low wide type with a pointed apex that, because it is wider than its height, gives a visual impression of having been flattened by the pressure above – hence the term 'depressed') that contains two small niches above it with three panels that contain shields. So it's not only impressive in design, it's also very intricate, with the intention of not only impressing first-time visitors but also reminding returning ones of the sheer gravity of the place they've travelled to.

Fittingly, it now serves as the main entrance to the priory grounds. And, maybe disappointingly, it may be that the modern visitor is so keen on getting inside and enjoying their walk and the views of the great arch of the ruined priory that lurks within, that, while looking for their admittance money with excited children dancing all around them, they completely forget or disregard the wonderful entrance that they are passing through – one that, if it was the lone attraction in any other village, would probably get more than its fair share of attention.

In Walsingham, however, it is just one more treasure in a village that is festooned with them, but, rightfully, it remains very modest and unassuming about its place in history, which makes it an absolute pleasure to visit.

(Ray Blyth)

Chapter 45

Walsingham

Water Pump

I wonder if this is the only medieval water pump you can find depicted on a fridge magnet, available (at the time of writing) from the Slipper Chapel shop for just £2.

Making the most of your marketable assets at religious shrines and places of worship is not just a symbol of these rampant commercial times, however. Medieval visitors to Walsingham would almost certainly have worn pilgrim badges to not only show where they were going and to be easily identifiable to fellow pilgrims, but in the same manner as wealthy merchants looked to secure their place in heaven by financing the construction of large wool churches, for example, pilgrims would have hoped their own modest devotion, marked by their pilgrimage and their very public 'badge of allegiance', would have earned them the same eternal rewards.

The badges were usually made of lead alloy and sold as souvenirs on the pilgrimage site itself. Each would have featured an image of the saint who was venerated at that particular location and, over time, and just as people smother their fridges today with the ubiquitous magnets, committed pilgrims would have amassed quite a collection of badges from all the well-known sites of religious devotion.

There is little difference, therefore, between buying a badge at Walsingham in the sixteenth century and purchasing a fridge magnet at the gift store today other than, of course, no self-respecting medieval tradesman would have dared produce a badge with an image on it that did not refer to the saint in question.

So what has the water pump in Walsingham done to deserve its place on a modern-day souvenir? Much of it is, of course, down to modern-day commercial tastes. Walsingham is a world-famous site and a very picturesque one, full of historical detail and old world charm. In such a location, a sixteenth-century octagonal pump house is going to merit some attention, particularly as it is in a prominent position in the village known as the Common Place.

A prominent feature on the pump house is the iron brazier that sits, fairly precariously, upon its stone roof. This was referred to locally as the 'beacon' and would, at one point, have been the only source of street lighting in the entire village, meaning that in medieval times, for all the spiritual light that would have emanated at Walsingham, it would at the dead of night have been a very dark place indeed. This must have made it as much a gathering place for the local thieves and muggers as for the pilgrims who would have been their prey. The brazier is still lit on special occasions, as it was when it became part of the chain of beacons that were lit around the country during the Queen's Diamond Jubilee celebrations in 2012.

The pump house was once also adorned with a pinnacle that was, sadly, never replaced after it was broken off in around 1900. Current opinion differs as to what was the cause of this particular act of vandalism (although, for once, we cannot blame the Reformation), but it is thought to have happened as a result of a rather extravagant application of bunting in and around it during either the celebrations for the Relief of Mafeking or the coronation of King Edward VII.

Clearly, the residents of Walsingham never let the village's status as a place of quiet devotion and prayer from stopping them having a good party.

(Ray Blyth)

Acknowledgements

No book of this nature could even begin to do its subject justice without the accompanying photographs for each and every site featured here. I am therefore indebted to all of the following for their kindness, co-operations and permissions given for their work to be included here:

David Dixon (www.geograph.org); Christine Matthews (www.geograph.org); BMA (www.shutterstock.com); Carmina McConnell (www.shutterstock.com); Adrian S.Pye (www.geograph.org.uk); Stephen McKay (www.geograph.org); Colin Cubitt (www.flickr.com); Diane Mower (www.shutterstock.com); John @APW (www.shutterstock.com); Julia Dowse (www.geograph.org.uk); Keith Evans (www.geograph.org.uk); Mark Newstead; Daniel Brigham at Norwich City FC; Ken Tidd; Mark Oakden (www.tournorfolk.co.uk); Hugh Venables (www.geograph.org); Nige Nudds (Nigel D. Nudds Photography); Peter Barr (www.geograph.org.uk); Richard Humphrey (www.geograph.org.uk); Stephen Bashford (www.geograph.org.uk); Caroline Davison at the Norfolk Archaeological Trust (www.norfarchtrust.org.uk); Patrick Phillips at Kentwell Hall (www.kentwell.co.uk) and Amy Taylor at the Landmark Trust (www.landmarktrust.org.uk).

With special thanks to Ray Blyth whose knowledge and passion for Follies in all their glory is unsurpassed. You can learn more about it at his website www.fabulousfollies.net.

The photograph of the water tower at Houghton Hall is reproduced with the kind permission of Lord Cholmondeley.

The wonderfully atmospheric painting of Seahenge on the beach at Holme is reproduced courtesy of Ken Hayes, you can find out more about Ken and his art at www.kenhayes.net.

Photographers, like all artists and people who work in the creative arts are, rightly, proud of their work so I do feel, with that in mind, it is also right to credit those photography platforms I have been able to explore and utilise separately, named www.flickr.com, www.shutterstock.com and www.geograph.org.uk.

If I have missed out else made an error with reference to these photographs and the photographers that took them, do rest assured that it was not intentional and that every effort has been made to ensure that the rights holder has been contacted and the correct permissions obtained. Please notify the publisher with the correct details so that a suitable correction can be included in future reprints of this book. Thank you.

Thanks also to the following people who have, in one way or another, helped with the planning and writing of this book: Russell Saunders for his thorough and very scrupulous approach to the art of proof reading. Margaret Ballard at the Aldeburgh Museum, Ray Couzens, Pete Goodrum, Heather Hamilton at Gressenhall Archaeology, Janet Lake and Sarah Povey.

And, finally, to the ever patient, understanding and infinitely agreeable Connor Stait and all at Amberley Publishing for their continued support in me and my work.

I am most grateful to you all.

Edward Couzens-Lake
www.couzenslakemedia.com